D0859838

PRAISE FOR *LEADING PEOPLE SAFELY*

"'I respect him who respects me.' This is one of the fundamental dynamics in *Leading People Safely*. In *Leading*, Schultz and Fielkow describe how to create an organization based upon trust and respect. Without trust and respect, our employees will not trouble themselves to report problems or unsafe conditions, and as is stated in *Leading*, 'Our front lines know where the real risks lie.'"

—Thomas Anthony
Director, Aviation Safety and Security Program,
University of Southern California

"Jim and Brian don't 'do' safety . . . they 'live' safety. Their book provides an invaluable road map for integrating safety into any organization using real-life examples of how large organizations have been transformed at their core. It's a great read for those who are struggling to instill a safety culture in their own organization."

—J. E. "Ed" Codd
Risk Management and Operating Executive, retired,
Ford Motor Company, CSX Corporation, and Waste
Management Inc.

"They say culture is what happens when the boss isn't watching! This would worry most executives, but not if you read Jim and Brian's book and implement as fast as you can. Jim and Brian's experiences and practical examples of how a leader brings integrity, vision, and empowerment to a team are unprecedented. You can't 'will' someone's desire to do the right thing. Tapping into this will and the desire in people to be extraordinary, not ordinary, is what Jim and Brian are all about. We're fortunate to have them share what 'winning' looks like."

—Kelly N. Cook, MBA
Chief Marketing Officer, Kmart
Harvard Business School's 2003 Dynamic Women in
Business Awardee

"Jim Schultz and Brian Fielkow are the leading professional practitioners in how to create a culture of positive safety in organizations today. The authors are not only knowledgeable of the fundamentals, but they also have years of experience successfully implementing these practices and philosophies in organizations of varied sizes and missions. As a career safety practitioner, I can attest to the value of this publication. It provides an effective road map on how to achieve world-class safety performance, zero safety failures, and transformation of your organization's morale, financial results, and customer satisfaction. This is a must read for anyone who is interested in benchmarking, assessing, and improving their organization's overall safety culture."

—John E. Fenton
President and CEO, Patriot Rail Company LLC

"These practitioners have hit the nail on the head. The tragedy of a poor safety culture is a leadership responsibility with far-blown implications, and the shop-floor employees will respond if they know that their safety and well-being are more important than production. Their response is shown in discretionary effort. I know this approach works, as I have seen it, lived it, and been changed by it."

—Stephen L. Goldman, MD
Corporate Medical Director, retired, Caterpillar Inc. and
CSX Corporation

"Fielkow and Schultz have over seventy-combined years of experience in organizational safety—to say that *Leading People Safely* represents that experience is an understatement. This book is more than the proverbial 'sum of its parts.' In fact, this book represents the lives of all those they have touched and saved over the course of two extraordinary careers."

—K. Scott Griffith
Founding Partner and Principal Collaborator, SG
Collaborative Solutions LLC

"During the years I worked at Waste Management Inc., I witnessed an organization transform itself from a poor safety record to a world-class leader in transportation safety. Along the way, I learned that improving safety is much more than regulatory compliance; it requires passionate leadership that creates a culture of safety—something to which many organizations aspire, but few attain. Jim is a true leader, and I am grateful for the time I spent with him. I use lessons every day that I learned from Jim, and I'm truly delighted that he and Brian have compiled their seventy-plus years of experience into a road map for others to follow."

—Ben Hoffman, MD
Global Chief Medical Officer, General Electric Oil & Gas
Adjunct Professor, University of Texas School of Public Health
Former VP and Chief Medical Officer, Waste Management Inc.
Former Chairperson, US Department of Transportation Federal Motor Carrier Safety Administration Medical Review Board

"Safety culture is a way of life and their central value. Jim Schultz and Brian Fielkow's book will guide your team step-by-step into this culture. These instilled values will at the same time grow good habits and accountability."

—Jerry Hominick
President and CEO, Hominick Custom Builders

"If your team doesn't already know the difference between priorities and values in safety, then this book is a must read. Jim Schultz and Brian Fielkow connect the 'journey to safety excellence' to both organizational achievement and financial performance, with compelling insight. The authors highlight, for example, how a safety culture is truly a just culture, where frontline operators in transport and industry ideally function in 'an atmosphere of trust in which people are encouraged or even rewarded for speaking up about mistakes or problems, but in which they are also clear about where the line must be drawn between acceptable and unacceptable behaviors.' As Jim and Brian put it, 'Safety is the cornerstone value in quality organizations.' With succinct anecdotes and strategies based on decades of public and private sector operational and management experience, this pivotal work outlines how safety aligns with enterprise success. Jim and Brian make clear that 'if you can't lead people safely, you can't lead people'—and this seminal but accessible and highly readable perspective belongs on the bookshelf of every leader."

—Donald M. Itzkoff
Executive Counsel, Government Affairs & Policy, GE Transportation, General Electric Company
Former Deputy Administrator, Federal Railroad Administration, US Department of Transportation
Former Senior Majority Counsel, US Senate Committee on Commerce, Science, and Transportation

"Safety failures by management and an individual led to the devastating loss of life that is felt every day by me and my children. We are not the only ones who have experienced such tragedy. Never underestimate the power of one. Please take the time to read this book and follow the provided guidelines. Make safety a nonnegotiable core value as well as your top daily individual priority!"

—Heidi Jenkins
International "Life Changer" Safety Advocate
Widow of Erich Jenkins

"The underlying premise that safety is not a priority is woven throughout this book with an impactful and elegant mix of theory and practice that extends far beyond a simple understanding of why safety is core to success, or even a plan or checklist for how to operationalize safety. Through their discussions, Jim and Brian engage the reader with the net result of instilling a way of thinking—a knowing of how to achieve safety performance."

—Katherine Andrea Lemos, PhD
Author, pilot, and aviation safety professional
Former Federal Aviation Administration (FAA) and
National Transportation Safety Board (NTSB) official

"I have been teaching and conducting research on safety culture for the last thirty years. However, this is the first time I came across such a lucidly written 'manual' on how to initiate, implement, operationalize, nurture, and sustain safety culture in an organization. This book ought to be assigned as a must read for leaders of safety-sensitive industries, most notably for its seminal conclusion, 'Who Packs Your Parachute?'"

—Dr. Najmedin Meshkati, PhD
Professor of Civil/Environmental Engineering,
Industrial & Systems Engineering, and International
Relations at the University of Southern California
Senior Science and Engineering Advisor, Office of
Science and Technology Advisor to the Secretary of
State, (2009–2010)

"When it comes to the essence of safety leadership, James Schultz and Brian Fielkow have nailed it with this book. As a NASA astronaut, I lived through the terrible days of the Challenger disaster and know what it's like to bury friends and colleagues and console their survivors . . . and to witness the destruction of a truly great team. And therein lies a critical message. If it can happen to a team that put six missions on the moon and returned the astronaut crews safely to Earth, it can happen to any team in any industry. Knowing this vulnerability to every organization, the authors have crafted this brilliant blueprint that leaders can employ to build a safety program that isn't just a value statement on a web page, but something alive and enduring within each team member. No leader, particularly those whose teams operate in hazardous environments, should be without this book."

—R. "Mike" Mullane
Astronaut, retired, STS-41D, STS-27, and STS-36, NASA

"Whether a leader in healthcare, transportation, manufacturing, or a service industry, this outstanding reference of practical and proven business wisdom belongs within easy reach during our daily professional endeavors. As I read this book, I compiled a list of colleagues and friends with whom I wish to share this gift."

—John W. Overton Jr., MD
Board-Certified in Emergency Medicine and
Cardiothoracic Surgery
Former Medical Officer, National Transportation Safety
Board (NTSB)

"Jim Schultz and Brian Fielkow have accomplished what other authors and safety practitioners have failed to do: bridge the gap between leadership, safety, and operations. Their book is a clear and concise outline on synchronizing culture and behavior so that leadership becomes an individual responsibility among all employees. The ability to place employee behavior and leadership at the center of a company's culture is key to consistent success. *Leading People Safely* is a book that accomplishes this and is a must read for all employees."

—Robert Pettit
Partner and Executive Vice President, The Presidio
Group

"Wow—another home run! Just as *Driving to Perfection* provided very practical steps on how to create a vibrant culture, *Leading People Safely* provides a blueprint on how to achieve safety excellence. Since implementing many of Brian's suggestions in *Driving to Perfection* over the past two years, we've enjoyed 35 percent organic growth. More importantly, virtually every quality metric has also improved as our culture has made dramatic improvements. I can't wait to implement the ideas Jim and Brian have put forth in this book. I'm sure we'll see our accident rates plummet over the next few years."

—Brad Pinchuk
CEO, Hirschbach Motor Lines Inc.

"Workplace and industrial safety is a topic that must be prominent in any business enterprise. All managers (executive or mid-level) and their employees must be able to not only talk freely about safety, but they must also be able to demonstrate it on a daily basis. This wonderful book, written so concisely by James T. Schultz and Brian L. Fielkow, is a must read and should be an addition to any library. It poignantly summarizes the needed perspectives of both management and labor in order for business to thrive in a teamwork sense . . . all while lives and property are safeguarded through a proactive safety program for any business."

—Timothy L. Smith
State Chairman, California State Legislative Board,
Brotherhood of Locomotive Engineers and Trainmen
Chairman, National Association of State Legislative
Board Chairmen

"Jim Schultz and Brian Fielkow have shared their lifetime of experience struggling to find a formula for a safe workplace. This book links culture to leadership with a constant need for reinforcement of safety values. This book also underscores the necessity to weave safety into the fabric of operations. Safety is not an item that can be checked off on our to-do list because safety is a part of every immediate demand on activities. I wish we had this [book] forty-five years ago when I witnessed my first fatality on the railroad. I sincerely hope this book becomes required reading for every manager and worker."

—James A. Stem Jr.
National Legislative Director, retired, United Transportation Union

"This book is a rich resource for all levels of leadership, for any sized team, for any industry. It is a rich compilation of principles . . . but it doesn't stop there. The authors inspire action with engaging personal examples, providing context that makes the principles memorable. These principles go beyond the workplace—they're tools for living. Read it and learn how to be an effective leader and an effective team member. You'll always remember that someone out there is packing your parachute."

—Leigh White
Executive Vice President, Corporate Development, CurAegis Technologies

"Trust and respect are necessary to truly inspire and engage a workforce to share their best ideas. I've found that people are compelled to share their best when they feel safe, both figuratively and literally. In *Leading People Safely: How to Win on the Business Battlefield*, Jim and Brian brilliantly point out how building a safety culture can help world-class organizations of all sizes perform to their fullest potential."

—Jim Whitehurst, President and CEO, Red Hat

"This is a straightforward book on how to make safety happen in your organization. I have seen firsthand how it can bring success in a very difficult environment where initially safety had no value whatsoever. In fact, the biggest lesson I learned was that it is impossible to achieve any kind of sustainable operational success if a company is blind to safety. Safety must be step one. Jim and Brian state it correctly. You cannot have a safety culture until everyone top to bottom realizes that it is not about what you do but who you are. Getting people involved at a visceral level, understanding the power of ownership and accountability, and committing themselves to consistently making the right choices are mandatory to getting a company onto a proper safety footing. If you have what it takes to take a company to new levels, this book should be on your desk day one."

—Charles E. "Chuck" Williams
Senior Vice President of Operations, retired, Waste
Management Inc.

LEADING

PEOPLE

SAFELY

LEADING PEOPLE SAFELY

HOW TO WIN ON THE BUSINESS BATTLEFIELD

JAMES T. SCHULTZ AND BRIAN L. FIELKOW

FOREWORD BY THE HONORABLE ROBERT L. SUMWALT, III

NORTH LOOP BOOKS

MINNEAPOLIS

NORTHLOOP
BOOKS

North Loop Books
322 First Avenue N, 5th floor
Minneapolis, MN 55401
612.455.2294
www.NorthLoopBooks.com

ISBN-13: 978-1-63505-136-0
LCCN: 2016910903

Distributed by Itasca Books

Cover Design by C. Tramell
Typeset by Mary Kristin Ross

Printed in the United States of America

CONTENTS

FOREWORD

It was shortly before seven on a Sunday morning when the phone rang. I had been sworn in as National Transportation Safety Board (NTSB) vice chairman just seven days earlier, and I certainly didn't think such a call would come so soon in my tenure. "Vice Chairman Sumwalt, please stand by while we connect the NTSB chairman," said the solemn voice from the NTSB's twenty-four-hour Response Operations Center.

In that brief conversation, the NTSB chairman told me the grim news: about an hour earlier, an airline crash occurred in Lexington, Kentucky. The aircraft was still burning. Multiple fatalities were suspected. I was to meet the NTSB "Go Team" at the airport and fly to Kentucky with them in a government jet. With that, I would begin a decade of being an NTSB board member, where I would witness firsthand the tragic consequences of good people ending up in bad situations. In the intervening decade, I deliberated over 150 transportation accidents. A common thread woven throughout many of these accidents was, at some level, the lack of effective safety leadership.

As I quickly learned, and as is discussed in this book, there is a real face to safety. The hardest, most difficult and painful conversations I had were with family members who were grieving the loss of a loved one following a transportation accident. Oftentimes I met with them within hours of the mishap, their emotions raw. The only sliver of inspiration I could offer at that point was my commitment to finding out what happened so that we could prevent it from happening again. But, as we all know, it would be far better to have prevented the accident in the first place. Preventing accidents is a core principle of safety leadership.

When it comes to safety leadership, there are academicians and there are practitioners. While there are some academics who have made truly profound advances in improving safety (Jim Reason and Najmedin Meshkati immediately coming to mind), there are those who are highly esoteric and theoretical. Theory doesn't always fly in the real-world business battlefield. I venture to guess that most practitioners, understandably, don't have time to translate theory into practice. Instead, they need tangible, workable, and understandable guidance.

Jim Schultz and Brian Fielkow, while quite scholarly in their own right, are mainly practitioners. They have been on the front lines of large, complex organizations, leading people safely to win on the business battlefield. They understand that good safety is good business. They have not just changed safety culture in organizations—they have actually transformed it. This book is a compilation of principles, practices, techniques, and ideas they have used in creating significantly safer work environments. The ingredients are all right here between the covers of this book. If a true commitment is made to implement them, a significant advance in safety will, almost certainly, emerge in your organization.

The title of this book was not chosen randomly or without thought. It was carefully chosen to illustrate the critical linkage between leadership and safety. An organization absent of leadership truly committed to running a safe operation, and absent of a workforce that truly believes and practices that commitment with everything they do, is an organization that is literally a place waiting for an accident to happen.

There is an age-old conflict between safety and production. If the scale is tipped too far in favor of production, catastrophe can occur; if the scale is tipped too far the other direction, production is sacrificed. Consider that perhaps the safest airline is probably one where the airplanes remain in the hangar and never fly. However, it wouldn't take long to figure out that the airline wouldn't make money, and if it didn't change the business model, it would quickly go out of business. On the other hand, if those airplanes flew all the time without regard to maintenance, weather conditions, crews scheduled to avoid fatigue, and airport capacity, it is doubtful the airline would remain in business very long due to actual or perceived problems with safety. I witnessed the perils of this firsthand.

Before my days at the NTSB, I spent a career as a pilot for a major US-based airline. In a five-year period, that airline experienced five fatal crashes. Following the fifth crash, *The New York Times* wrote a scathing (but fairly accurate) article about the airline and its safety problems. The airline later attributed a loss of at least $150 million in revenue—not attributed to the actual crashes, but simply to the negative publicity brought about by the article. The following quarter, the airline's auditors, KPMG Peat Marwick LLP, issued an opinion expressing "substantial doubt about [the airline's] ability to continue as a going concern." Once an organization loses the trust of its customers, once people question the company's safety, customers go elsewhere. The airline had an excellent route structure, but the best of business models are easily undermined by a perceived lack of safety. Just as good safety is good business, a bad safety record is bad for business.

In addition to the financial cost associated with lack of safety leadership, there is an underappreciated cost, as well—the cost of employee morale and well-being. One of the ill-fated flights departed from my hometown, Columbia, South Carolina, and crashed while on approach to Charlotte, North Carolina. Because the flight originated in Columbia, thirty-four of the thirty-seven fatalities were from the Columbia area. A few days after the crash, I was jogging along my usual route, wearing a T-shirt with the name of my airline written in large, bright colors across the front. As I was waiting to cross a busy street, a funeral procession passed by. I remember the shame I experienced, wondering if the funeral was for someone killed on my airline. In the ensuing months, I was actually ashamed to tell people which airline I flew for. People began referring to the airline, not by its actual name, USAir, but as "US Scare."

So, despite the conflict between safety and production, safety must always be set to win. Otherwise, there are enormous financial and human tolls as consequence for when things don't go well. That said, those of us in the safety business know it's hard to measure the accidents that didn't happen. Despite that difficulty, the authors have a track record that truly measured just that: the dollar benefit of accidents prevented. As detailed in this book, they were able to save their organization $75 million annually in workers' compensation costs. How did they do it? By leading people safely.

The formula is all right here in this book, and there are several key ingredients. Allow me to highlight two of them: safety culture and values.

There are many definitions and attributes of safety culture and the authors do a very nice job addressing them. When speaking to groups about safety leadership, I oftentimes ask a simple question: do you have a good safety culture? Although a simple question, the answer can be complex. I encourage participants to carefully consider their answer and to keep their reply to themselves. I suspect every audience has a few who feel smug, overly confident that they are doing all the right things. I pity them. To quickly shake them from a potentially dangerous misconception,

I show the participants a quote by Professor Jim Reason: "It is worth pointing out that if you are convinced that your organization has a good safety culture, you are almost certainly mistaken. . . . A good safety culture is something that is striven for but rarely attained. . . . [And] the process is more important than the product."

Dr. Reason's statement is profound in many ways. It provides a cautionary tale that once we feel we are "there," we tend to get complacent. Once complacency sets in, we lose focus on operating safely. In his writings, Reason mentions a "chronic unease" that, although perhaps unsettling, keeps us alert to potential safety problems. Complacency is truly an enemy on the business battlefield. Reason's quote also makes the point that there is no "there" with safety culture. Like safety itself, there is no destination; it's the constant journey—the processes and the struggles associated with it—that keeps us on our toes.

As illustrated in this book, perhaps the most important aspect of safety leadership is having an organizational culture where the organization possesses, as the US Nuclear Regulatory Commission defines safety culture, "the core values and behaviors resulting from a collective commitment by leaders and individuals to emphasize safety over competing goals to ensure protection of people and the environment." Although this system of beliefs and practices must permeate the entire organization, it squarely starts with top-level leadership.

In 2009, the nation's capital was rocked by a tragic subway accident. A subway train ran into the rear of a standing train at approximately forty-eight miles per hour. Given that the crash occurred at the height of rush hour, casualties were high. Nine lives were lost, and dozens more [passengers] were hospitalized. During the NTSB's investigative hearing, the chairman of the Washington Metropolitan Area Transit Authority (WMATA), the organization that operated the subway, testified that safety culture begins at the bottom of the organization and works its way up the chain. I emphatically disagreed with that assertion then, and I strongly disagree with it now. Make no mistake about it: putting pieces in place to form a healthy safety culture is a leadership function. Given the WMATA chairman's misplaced belief about where safety begins, there should be no irony that, based on overwhelming evidence discovered in the investigation, the NTSB determined a contributing factor in the accident was "WMATA's lack of a safety culture." Also listed as a contributing factor was "ineffective safety oversight by the WMATA Board of Directors." Indeed, safety must begin at the top. It is a leadership function to ensure the right message is developed, delivered, understood, and practiced.

Even if top leadership truly wants a healthy safety culture, oftentimes the message gets distorted somewhere between the top-level management and the frontline employees. The NTSB investigated five accidents involving Metro-North Railroad that occurred in an eleven-month period between May 2013 and March 2014. Operating in and out of New York City with destinations into New York State, New Jersey, and Connecticut, Metro-North is one of the largest and busiest commuter railroads in the US. As part of the investigative process, NTSB investigators handed out an attitudinal survey to Metro-North employees. Of the 156 surveys returned, twenty-five were from management, and the remaining 131 were from labor. One statement on the survey was: "Management is committed to workplace safety and participates regularly in safety events." The responses were quite telling: those by senior and middle management were quite positive, while those provided by labor offered a completely divergent perspective. There were similarly disparate responses with other survey questions as well, such as, "Management does not pressure staff to maintain services or operations, potentially at the cost of safety."

Perhaps the dissonance in these attitudes grew over time. Decades earlier, Metro-North was the darling of commuter railroads, operating proudly in and out of New York's Grand Central Terminal. But, slowly, things must have changed. Perhaps management grew smug. Perhaps they grew complacent. Perhaps they relied on a past record of no accidents to mistakenly believe they were better than they really were. Whatever the reasons, the safety of the railroad came sharply into focus in May 2013, when two commuter trains sideswiped each other following a derailment. There were no fatalities, but the accident raised important questions about Metro-North's rail inspection and maintenance. That same month a rail maintenance worker was killed when a rail dispatcher mistakenly routed a train into a work zone that should have been off-limits to trains. On December 1, 2013, a sleep-deprived locomotive engineer dozed off at the controls and failed to slow for a sharp curve. Traveling at eighty-two miles per hour over a curve that had a speed limit of thirty miles per hour, the train hurtled off the tracks, spewing rail cars and debris over a section of the Bronx. Four lives were lost.

The NTSB's investigative hearing received testimony from the railroad's president. He stated he never wanted any employee to compromise safety for any reason, including on-time performance. Judging from his passion, he probably meant it. But, the survey results mentioned above, as well as other statements by front-line employees, painted an entirely different picture. Regardless of what management said they wanted, the frontline employees "heard" something else. Quite simply, there was a lack of alignment between management and employees. I venture to say that lack of alignment in goals and values is one of the greatest dysfunctions of an organization. Achieving that alignment is a critical function of safety leadership and is a focus of this book.

Alignment begins with values. I believe there are two types of organizations—those that truly live their values and those that don't. Sadly, in many cases value statements are just words hanging on the wall, on a web page, or peppering a company's annual report. Other than that, they are basically unknown or not practiced.

I once was involved in an organization that spent copious amounts of time and effort developing organizational values. You probably know the drill—retreat after retreat, scores of butcher paper hanging on the walls with Magic Marker scribble, bleary-eyed workshops and discussions. After much finagling, the values were approved and rolled out to the entire workforce in person and via webcast. But, after all of the handshaking and the big proclamation of values, nothing changed. More than a year after the values were announced, the organization's intranet still displayed the old values. Decisions were made and actions performed that were incongruent with the values. Discouraged, I suggested to the head of the organization that we weren't living our values. He replied, "Oh, I disagree—I think we are doing all of those things." However, successful organizations don't *do* their values—they *live* them with everything they do. Each decision, action, and intended action should be measured against those values to make sure you are being true to them.

Chapter 2 of this book describes the difference between values and priorities. As the authors point out, priorities come and go. Values, on the other hand, are the fabric of the organization. They don't change unless a great deal of thought and wrangling has gone into it. With that framework, think about the number of times you've heard or seen so-called leaders proclaim that "safety is our top priority." This worn-out cliché usually signals rhetoric without substance. Safety should not merely be a priority— it must be a value. It must be lived and practiced with everything you do.

A powerful example of an organization living and practicing their values was illustrated by CVS Health. CVS is, of course, the familiar chain of nearly eight thousand pharmacies that dot street corners of communities across America. In February 2014, CVS announced they would discontinue sale of tobacco products. Although this decision would cause CVS to forgo an estimated $2 billion in annual revenue, the CEO of CVS stated at the time, "The sale of tobacco products is inconsistent with our purpose—helping people on their path to better health." Following the announcement, Dr. Michael Woody commented, "This move is clearly in-line with their stated purpose and values, a move we don't see often enough today in corporate America. Relying on a strong foundation of values is often what sets market leaders apart from the pack. Think of values as the core guiding principles that act as the foundation of your organization. These principles should guide every decision and serve as your fallback in times of uncertainty."

How has this decision to live their values affected CVS's financial performance? Despite losing potential revenue from tobacco sales, CVS ended 2014—the year the decision was made to end such sales—with $139.4 billion in revenue, a 10 percent revenue increase over 2013. Furthermore, in the two years since CVS made this announcement, its stock increased 37 percent. This outperformed the New York Stock Exchange, where CVS stock is traded, which had declined 6 percent during this same period. It also outperformed the Dow Jones Industrial Average, which increased by a scant 2 percent during those two years. Furthermore, CVS's stock outperformed its two main competitors', who, incidentally, did not undertake the bold value-based decision that CVS did.

Does this mean that living your values will automatically increase your organization's financial performance? Probably not. However, it may signal that organizations with strong leaders are those organizations that ensure their values are aligned and lived throughout the organization. They do the right things by caring for the safety and health of their employees and customers. Because of their commitment to values and caring, they have greater potential to perform well financially.

In closing, this book provides a roadmap for safety leadership. I encourage you to read each chapter with an open mind. As you read, think of ways to apply the information in your organization. While some of this may be easy, be prepared that some may be difficult. But, rest assured that your efforts to implement these ideas can mean the difference between winning and losing on the business battlefield. As leaders, you not only have the *ability* to influence safety, but you have the *obligation* to do so, as well. I wish you great success.

The Honorable Robert L. Sumwalt III
Columbia, South Carolina
February 2016

PREFACE:

Our Thesis

Our thesis is that the leadership skills required to successfully lead safety are the same skills needed to lead outstanding operations: attention to detail, focused execution, standardized and disciplined processes, understanding of roles, meaningful metrics, personal accountability, and alignment around the group vision and mission. These qualities are the "bricks and mortar" that structure the culture and provide the tangible order necessary to drive results. In substance, we have four foundational beliefs:

1. The best action an organization can take to align and engage employees is to make them feel valued. A culture of positive safety does just that.

2. A journey to safety excellence has to be a crusade, not a casual endeavor. People will not normally evolve to change of this magnitude. It must be deliberate, with a crafted process and messaging.

3. There must be energy around the vision. Process alone will not affect the level of change needed.

4. This journey must be leadership driven. It can't be delegated.

Building and maintaining a culture of positive safety is a journey worth taking. Great safety secures a competitive advantage in a highly aggressive marketplace. The fate of the organization may rely on how well the team functions, and how well the team functions is a direct outcome of leadership.

This is not a book of scientific research, academic theses, or imposing statistics. Rather, in this book we offer our personal perspective through real-life experiences and observations over seventy-plus years of combined tenure in organizational trenches, in both private and public sector organizations, from entry level positions to the C-suite, from tiny entities to enormous corporations. From the outset, we want to make clear that we are not safety experts, nor does either one of us hold professional safety certifications. We are safety practitioners. We have seen safety in living color at the ground level. Far from theoretical, our views expressed in this text are views forged through experience. We have witnessed good safety leaders, poor safety leaders, and everything in between.

What follows in this book are our opinions and advice on what works, what doesn't work, and how you can be a more effective leader—not just in safety, but in every aspect of governing your company, organization, department, or team. After all if you can't lead people safely, you can't lead people. Great safety is the foundation for great customer engagement, financial performance, and operational excellence.

INTRODUCTION:

It's Time to Take a New Approach to Safety and Accident Prevention

Safety is the decisive component in the social DNA of best-in-class companies. That is a bold statement, to be sure. In this book we will explain why we believe that safety is as close to the proverbial "silver bullet" as you can find that enables a company to achieve and sustain highly reliable performance, maximum financial results, and outstanding operations.

A culture of positive safety is a driver of employee engagement—a key constituent of top-tier performance. When people feel that management cares about them as individuals, they willingly reciprocate with differential effort that propels companies ahead of competitors. This can be the ultimate advantage for any business, especially those that are service driven.

An investment in safety is an investment in your bottom line. Safety is the foundation of an excellent business operation, and leaders who ignore or delegate safety are jeopardizing organizational profitability and longevity. Building a safe company is not about more rules and regulations. It is about building a behavior-based culture.

Moreover, safe and environmentally sound social governance is a public expectation. James O'Toole and Warren Bennis perhaps said it best: "It appears that the new metric of corporate leadership will be closer to this: *the extent to which executives create organizations that are economically, ethically, and socially sustainable*."

To create a business environment that is both safe and

profitable, we need to change how we think about safety. Each year, we witness via mass media the major automobile and truck accidents, plane crashes, and train derailments. These are only the tip of the iceberg of the numerous safety failures that are not in the public eye and therefore never make the news. The list of safety failures that normally do not make the news is as long as the imagination will allow. They include slips, trips, and falls; forklift accidents; faulty product design or manufacture; or security breaches in an office building. We have a transportation background and will refer to personal examples throughout this book. That said, this is *not* a book about transportation safety. The principles and practices in this book apply to leading people safely in any business or industry.

Government regulation and our voluminous handbooks can go only so far in implementing a safety culture. Personal choice takes us the rest of the way. The only way companies can influence personal choice is by creating a safety culture within every facet of their business. When it comes to safety, it's less about rules and regulations and more about managing behavior and realizing that safety is not a cost—it's a strategic choice with profound bottom-line results. In doing this, we must abandon antiquated thinking about safety and embrace what *really* drives safe outcomes in our businesses.

As leaders, we must demonstrate, teach, and manage acceptable safety behaviors. An injury or fatality does not just happen. It is most likely the result of a series of unsafe behaviors that went unaddressed.

Not only must we hold our employees individually accountable for safety results, but we must also create organizational accountability. It is quick and easy to blame an individual. It requires greater courage and discipline to look for shortcomings in your own organization that may be the real reason for a safety failure.

As business leaders, we have an obligation to create the safest possible environment for our employees and the public. If you think an investment in safety is too expensive, consider the opposite. Ignoring safety ultimately will lead to accidents, litigation, increased insurance costs, product failures, damaged reputations, poor employee morale, and, eventually, business failure.

Customers: Why Safety Matters

Ignoring safety will cost your business long term in the modern era, and putting safety on the back burner will hinder your ability to grow. Smart customers now perform due diligence on their vendors. In our experience, more and more good companies, the kind you want as customers, are basing their business decisions on safety performance. Nobody wants rogue operators in their facilities or handling their products. Reputation, brand quality, and service are big deals to customers. Everybody wants their brand to be associated with winners. Said another way, few customers want their name to be linked with poor-quality performers in the public domain. Safe, clean, responsible conduct—not necessarily price—will often be the element that determines if a customer will hire you or someone else.

For example, Brian's transportation company, Jetco Delivery, depends on providing their shippers safe, efficient, and on-time product shipment. It is core to their business. Shippers select transportation partners carefully and will pay a premium to do business with safe, cordial, and efficient companies. They depend upon their transportation providers to deliver their products to their customers undamaged and in a safe, efficient manner. They don't want their products in the hands of careless people unable to fulfill their commitments to their customers. They also want a vendor partner who will be prepared if anything goes wrong, with proper insurance levels, transparent communi-cations, and detailed root cause analyses. A healthy safety culture is job security at this most basic level for those who manage customer products and reputation.

It is difficult to provide a safe, cordial, and efficient customer experience if your frontline people are not engaged and aligned around your safety vision. More-over, ignoring safety will destroy employee morale. Your employees understand that an investment in safety is an investment in their well-being. The best option to engage employees is to show them you care. Putting employee safety front and center demonstrates management's commitment to people. It reaps tangible benefits (reduced costs and improved productivity) and intangible benefits (engendered employee loyalty) for any group. Employees reciprocate by giving that differential effort back to the organization and its customers. It is the ultimate win-win environment. Show us a world-class, highly productive, and profitable company, and we'll show you a company that cares for employees and values safety.

Safety is not something that we can delegate. If we make safety a low priority, the rest of the organization will follow our lead. If safety is confined to a department, it will never take hold throughout the organization. A safety department can coach, train, and mentor, but only an oper-ationally aligned organization can execute on safety with excellence. Safety execution requires a different and vastly broader approach than regulatory compliance. It must be driven by company leadership and anchored to the front line.

Let's abandon the notion that business leaders are smarter than our front lines when it comes to safety. Our front lines know where the real risks lie. They have the answers, if we would just listen. We need to make a commitment to bring our frontline leadership into the process and truly listen to and learn from our subject-matter experts and opinion leaders.

We hear organizations say, "Safety is our top priority." That isn't good enough. Knowing the difference between values and priorities is the single greatest point of confusion for an organization. Values define and bind us together, drive decisions in every interaction, and never change. Priorities are tasks requiring action, must be managed daily, and shift frequently based on a given situation. We must ensure that values are never compromised. Safety, and safe behaviors, must be nonnegotiable values in our businesses.

In summary, we don't need more rules and regulations. Instead, we need greater safety leadership starting from the top of our organizations. Safety excellence, after all, is simply a subset of an operationally excellent company. It starts with each leader and then is owned by the employees.

PART I:

The Foundation: Principles for Creating a World-Class Safety Culture

CHAPTER 1:

What Is Culture, and Why Is It Important?

In its simplest terms, culture is the convergence of people and process. Culture is the bone marrow of an organization. It is the adhesive that joins an organization together. Research and experience have established that culture can be the ultimate differentiator in any enterprise. Companies with a success culture have a competitive advantage. Having engaged people vested in organizational success is the hardest component for a competitor to replicate. On the other hand, a poor culture most certainly undermines performance, marginalizes financial returns, and jeopardizes long-term viability.

An excellent culture occurs when people and process are in harmony with the company's vision and values. When this happens, employees are empowered and engaged—they share the same beliefs and values as the company and agree with its way of operating. Accepted patterns of behavior are clearly expressed and understood, and, ultimately, customers enjoy positive experiences in their interactions with the company.

Culture is:
- a unique group identity based upon shared beliefs and values;
- empowered employees doing what is right;
- accepted patterns of behavior;
- a hard-core business proposition; and
- process driven.

Above all, culture is a strategic choice.
A vibrant culture will not develop in an autocratic environment where decisions flow from the top down. Employees who are not empowered are simply not engaged in their jobs.

Consider this simple truth: *At its core, your company's culture is behavior based. It is a mix of individual and organizational behavior, all of which is functioning in alignment with your company's values.*

Safety Climate and Safety Culture

When applying this concept in a safety context, it is prudent to understand the concepts of safety climate and safety culture. We have encountered managers who incorrectly think that the two terms are transposable. In substance, safety climate is a temporal condition. It describes employee perceptions of what is important at a given place and time. Like the environmental conditions outside, safety climate is highly variable and subject to change as situations evolve. Safety culture, on the other hand, encompasses the long-term values of an organization. While the safety climate will change as situations and group priorities change, the underlying organizational safety culture will not change. Don't let your organization confuse the two concepts.

A culture of positive safety is not a destination. It is not something that you achieve then go on to the next challenge. As a leader, once you think your company is "there," you most certainly are setting yourself up for dysfunctional creep that can make your culture sick. Building and sustaining a culture of positive safety is a journey that never ends. It requires nurturing with continuous leadership focus. The sixteenth-century theologian Martin Luther, referring to the Reformation, once said, "We are not yet what we shall be, but we are growing toward it. The process is not yet finished, but it is going on. This is not the end, but it is the road." So it is with the journey to a positive safety culture. The real benefit is that the journey itself will drive success. Striving to get better every day provides energy that powers improvement.

CHAPTER 2:

Safety is Not a Priority—It's a Core Value

As Brian pointed out in *Driving to Perfection*, confusing values and priorities will create a lack of clarity among the team. This is especially important in the context of building a vibrant safety culture. Values define us and bind us together, drive decisions in all our interactions, and never change. Priorities, on the other hand, are tasks requiring action, must be managed daily, and shift frequently based on a given situation. However, even though priorities are the starting points for your day-to-day activities, your values should always guide your actions. Understand that people often do not properly differentiate values from priorities. You must ensure that broad-based understanding exists within your company, and that—while your priorities may shift—your values are never compromised.

Although priorities may vary from person to person and from day to day, on a winning team everyone has knowledge of—and is committed to—the same values.

Teams function best when there are clear, consistent, and inviolable values. These values are the guardrails that keep the organization steady during times of challenge. We can't talk about safety once in a while or only when an incident is in front of us. We talk about, think about, and strategize about safety every day.

We are often invited to present workshops on workplace safety to other business leaders. Our public talks provide an ample opportunity to reflect on the most effective tools to promote and maintain safety within a vibrant culture and successful business. Over time, we have organized and shaped what we believe are the most effective approaches for creating a safety culture.

A healthy safety culture is nothing more than a subset of a healthy overall culture. A healthy safety culture cannot grow inside a broken organizational culture. It's not possible.

Unfortunately, many leaders take a short-sighted view about safety. They regard safety as a cost, not as an investment. Then, when safety failures occur, they look for somebody to blame, or they rush in to establish more rules and regulations. While such a knee-jerk reaction may yield some benefit, it pales in comparison to the effectiveness of building a true culture of prevention as the bedrock of any organization. So take heed of this critical lesson: *a successful business is one that builds a safety culture, not a cost culture.*

You cannot build a safe organization without the same focus on culture. Culture is behavior. Culture is about doing what is right when nobody's looking.

What is at the root cause of every preventable accident? It's a failure to appreciate the risk at hand. Many of us wear tennis shoes from a company whose slogan is "Just Do It." In a safety-sensitive business, "just do it" doesn't work. We need to carefully plan before we execute. Safety is about prevention and anticipating what can go wrong.

In the old school, safety and operations were at war. In the new school, safety and operations are one and the same.

As business leaders, we must create the safest possible environment for our employees, our customers, and the public. That should be our driving force, not concern over government, industry rules, or insurance issues and the costs involved in strictly adhering to them. We need to live, breathe, and communicate this value.

For many business leaders, committing to a culture of prevention is a new way of acting at every level. It's more than simply bringing in more advanced safety-related training. It's a philosophy, an attitude. It resets the gauge and recalibrates organizational priorities.

A culture of prevention is a subset of your overall healthy and vibrant culture. As it relates specifically to safety, your company culture should be designed to nurture accident prevention by hiring and integrating the right people, eliminating behavior that contributes to accidents happening, and weaving the right processes into your company's DNA. By doing this, safety and safe behaviors will permeate your entire company.

CHAPTER 3:

People Value Most What They Cannot Buy

Nobody cares how much you know
until they know how much you care.
—attributed to Theodore Roosevelt

There is enough research to state with some certainty that, in general, job satisfaction isn't always about the money. While important to pay the bills, money can't buy what people value most:

- Money can buy schooling—*but not wisdom.*
- Money can buy a bed—*but not sleep.*
- Money can buy a clock—*but not time.*
- Money can buy a gift—*but not friendship.*
- Money can buy medicine—*but not health.*
- Money can buy social status—*but not respect.*
- Money can buy nice things—*but not a happy home.*

We have listed, below, the results of the comprehensive *Global Benchmarking Employee Engagement Study* by Right Management from December 2008. This comprehensive study reports findings from research into key drivers of employee engagement of nearly thirty thousand workers at all levels in fifteen countries. The results provide compelling evidence that people value most the things they cannot buy.

Top Global Engagement Drivers
1.   I am committed to my organization's core values.

2. Our customers think highly of our products and services.
3. My opinion counts.
4. I have a clear understanding of what is expected of me at work.
5. I understand how I can contribute to meeting the needs of our customers.
6. I have been fairly rewarded.
7. Senior leaders value employees.
8. Everyone is treated with respect at work, regardless of who they are.
9. I can concentrate on my job when I am at my work area.
10. My personal work objectives are linked to my work area's business plan.

While the 2008 Right Management study may seem dated, more current research affirms similar findings. For example, from August 2014 to August 2015, the group TINYpulse conducted a study focused on employee satisfaction with their careers that had over four hundred thousand responses from people in five hundred different organizations. Their findings were convincing. For instance, they reported that 78 percent of today's business leaders rate engagement and retention as one of their top concerns. In all, they found seven major trends impacting workplaces around the world:

1. *Never Underestimate Culture*: Culture drives happiness. Some of the strongest factors correlated to employee happiness include work environment and organizational culture.

2. *Peers and Colleagues Rule*: The #1 thing that employees love about their workplaces is their peers and colleagues.

3. *Attrition Is Around the Corner*: Believe it or not, nearly one in four employees would leave their workplaces if offered a 10% raise elsewhere.

4. *Professional Growth Is Lacking*: A mere 25% of employees note strong opportunities for professional growth—troubling news for millennial-rich workplaces with employees that crave these opportunities.

5. *No One Feels Valued or Appreciated*: Not even one in three employees feels strongly valued thanks to managers failing to show appreciation or, worse yet, constantly pointing out faults.

6. *Employees Don't Feel They're Meeting Their Potential*: Over 70% of all employees don't see themselves meeting their full potential. Some cite their own future growth, but nearly a quarter cite running around putting out fires instead of being truly focused.

7. *Lack of Colleague Follow-Through Kills Productivity*: 35% of all employees cite lack of follow-through and communication from colleagues as the top things that destroy productivity at work. (The TINYpulse 2015 Employee Engagement & Organizational Culture Report)

The bottom-line message in all of this research affirms that famous cliché and what we all intuitively know: people will forget what you do, they will forget what you say, but they will never forget how you make them feel. Think about what really matters. Ask someone to name the last five Super Bowl MVPs, the last five Nobel Peace Prize winners, or even the last five best actor Academy Award winners. These are all big-news items covered extensively in the media. Yet, chances are, no one will be able to answer.

Now, ask someone to tell you about a teacher or friend who helped in tough times, or a person who inspired and made him or her feel better. Everyone has an immediate answer. The lesson here is that it isn't always the most famous or the most renowned people who make a difference. It is those who care about you as an individual. This can be the magic of leadership, too. This translates into better results all around.

Keep the Three Ts Alive and Well

To engender an employee-owned safety culture it is essential that the "Three Ts" are alive and well. Without the Three Ts, employees will not be properly engaged. If employees are not engaged, they are less likely to own responsibility for safety.

As Brian discusses in *Driving to Perfection*, treatment, transparency, and trust are the fundamental pillars of a healthy manager-employee relationship. Data have shown that transparency is the number-one driver of employee happiness. Why? Because it fosters healthy relationships and trust between leaders and their teams. Holding periodic one-to-one meetings between managers and their direct reports, as well as monthly company meetings, can go a long way in cultivating positive workplace cultures where employees thrive and are aligned with the company's mission. Ensure that your managers make time to learn about their team members as individuals, that they share key data and information points regularly, and that their words and actions line up. Upholding the Three Ts will promote a healthy manager-employee relationship; when this relationship is solid, aligned and safe behaviors are much more likely to result.

Treatment

It only makes sense that an employee will not truly own his or her work if treated poorly. When we think of poor treatment, we think of the obvious examples: rudeness, profanity, etc. The real examples of poor treatment are much subtler and more destructive.

Poor treatment manifests itself through a failure of management to treat an employee as a human being first and an employee second. The employee is viewed as a number. Management does not listen to or dismisses employee concerns or ideas. When a manager exhibits these behaviors, he or she is telling that employee that the employee is not important. This type of poor treatment leads the employee to believe that he or she is anonymous and does not matter. An employee who believes that he or she doesn't matter will not embrace safe behaviors or other core company values.

Transparency

You know that sinking feeling: "I just work here. Management makes decisions, and it doesn't matter if I agree or disagree." If employees believe that everything happens behind closed doors, they will be disconnected from the desired safety behaviors and outcomes that the company seeks to promote.

This common perception often results from a lack of transparency. To promote a culture of transparency, sometimes it is as simple as explaining the "why." Take the time to let your employees know why decisions were made. Always remember: If people understand the "why," they are likely to support the process. If people are left in the dark, they are likely to oppose the process.

Trust

A 2015 Edelman corporate reputation report quoted a recent Watson Wyatt research finding that revealed a stunning fact: companies with high employee trust levels outperform those with low trust levels by 186 percent (based on three-year total shareholder return). This is a remarkable endorsement for why treating people in a just manner helps build trust. If your workers know that they won't be punished for unintentional errors, they will develop trust. That correlates to big financial benefits.

Stephen R. Covey made the point that with the increasing focus on ethics in our society, the character side of trust is fast becoming the price of entry into the new global economy. "The differentiating and often ignored side of trust—competence—is . . . essential. You might think a person is sincere, even honest, but you won't trust that person fully if he or she doesn't get results. And the opposite is true. A person might have great skills and talents and a good track record, but if he or she is not honest, you're not going to trust that person either." Covey goes on to describe twelve common behaviors of trusted leaders around the world that build and allow them to maintain trust. "Remember that the 12 Behaviors always need to be balanced by each other (e.g., Talk Straight needs to be balanced by Demonstrate Respect, etc.) and that any behavior pushed to the extreme can become a weakness."

1. Listen First and Talk Straight

2. Demonstrate Respect

3. Create Transparency

4. Right Wrongs

5. Show Loyalty

6. Deliver Results

7. Get Better

8. Confront Reality

9. Clarify Expectations

10. Practice Accountability

11. Keep Commitments

12. Extend Trust

If treatment or transparency is lacking in your company, trust will surely suffer. Without trust, your company will be unable to build vibrant safety culture. Motives and actions will always be doubted. Employees will work against each other instead of as a team. Trust is your most precious asset and is at the foundation of your ability to manage your company's safety performance. With trust, employee ownership of all aspects of their careers, including safety execution, will grow.

CHAPTER 4:

Know Accountability—Know Safety

When we teach business leaders and managers how to create and sustain a vibrant culture through our workshops and other presentations, we emphasize the need to look out for the common culture killers. High on that list is a lack of accountability. You simply can't build a safety culture and a successful business without solid, consistent accountability throughout your company. Accountability is fundamental to your mission. Accountability is the only way to ensure your front lines own safety. It is easy to preach accountability, but it is often difficult to put it into practice.

Let's recognize that accountability comes in three flavors:

1. Individual Accountability

2. Organizational Accountability

3. Peer-to-Peer Accountability

Promoting accountability on all three fronts helps ensure that your entire team is working together to take responsibility for all of your operations. It ensures that people at all levels of the organization take pride in what they do and own the results. With accountability, they're not afraid of making mistakes, but when errors or misjudgments emerge they step up to address them thoroughly without fear of consequences.

To fully understand accountability, consider what a *lack* of accountability looks like in all three realms:

Lack of Individual Accountability:
- Employees know their jobs but choose not to execute them completely or consistently.

- Employees are quick to pass the buck to another person or department.

- Employees are not sure what course of action to take but make no effort to seek clarification before going forward.

- Employees operate from a parent-child mentality, just looking to or waiting for management to tell them what they did wrong.

Lack of Organizational Accountability:

- Leaders and managers accept bad behavior and tolerate excuses.

- Management defends questionable actions or attitudes with the explanation, "We've always done it this way."

- Management makes demands that are not reasonable.

- Processes and procedures do not exist or are not understood.

- Outcomes are not tied to results, with no consequences for poor results and no rewards for excellent results.

Lack of Peer-to-Peer Accountability:

- Employees see something inappropriate in the actions or behavior of a peer but hold back from saying anything to that person due to a fear of how he or she will react.

- Employees look the other way when they witness inappropriate behavior by a peer because, "That's management's problem."

- Employees are convinced that if they go out of their way to actualize peer-to-peer accountability, no one on their team will like them.

Lack of accountability is often triggered by a general avoidance of confrontation or a human tendency to deny messing up. It is important to identify where your organization falls short of accountability. Review those three lists, adding other signs of non-accountability that you may see, and zero in on those areas that point to the issues sabotaging your company and your culture. It may be time for a course correction.

What Can You Do to Encourage Greater Individual Accountability?

Make sure that management does not cultivate an environment of workplace blame. If your employees believe that management is quick to blame, they are less likely to take responsibility for their actions. They're afraid of someone lowering the boom on them. Help employees understand and trust that those who act recklessly or who take deliberate and unjustifiable risks will face consequences, but those who make an understandable or unintentional mistake will not be punished. The emphasis instead will be on learning from the error and taking any necessary follow-up action.

This approach is consistent with treating your employees with respect, remembering that they are human beings first and employees second. We all make mistakes. Facing them takes courage and commitment, and it's easier for employees to summon those traits when they know they are trusted and will be treated fairly.

Also, highlight the importance of asking questions. Explain that they have a choice of operating in a sea of uncertainty or asking for clarification. Once they are clear on expectations and procedures, they are less likely to make mistakes or fear admitting to them.

When people ask, "How can I become more accountable?" it's a serious question. This is a question asked by an individual who wants to improve. Here are a few ideas that will increase accountability:

- **Be self-aware. It starts with you.** You must be aware of how you show up. Culture starts with you, and you are responsible for your actions and understanding the impact they have on everyone around you—from your coworkers to your customers.

- **You set the tone. You create the environment.** Show up ready to go and to put your best foot forward. A Chinese proverb states, "The people follow the example of those above them." The way you show up and interact sets the tone for the situation. Don't let the inevitable setbacks tarnish your outlook. Stay the course.

- **Attitude is everything.** Choose how you're going to respond. Come with a good attitude. Customers and coworkers don't want to deal with a bad attitude, and they won't. Customers will go somewhere else.

- **Determine how to manage stress and conflict.** Find an outlet for stress. An unhealthy level of stress can harm your attitude and passion for your work. That is certain to impact your accountable behavior. Take a walk; take a break; go to a quiet room; talk to a coworker, friend, or loved one; go to the gym. Seek outside help if necessary. Figure out what works for you.

- **Treat everyone with the same level of importance. Don't play the organization chart.** Be consistent in your actions. Don't act one way in front of one person and another way in front of someone else. For example, when you're in front of upper management, don't take a particular attitude, then turn around and do the opposite in front of your peers.

Let's expand a bit on the first concept—be self-aware. It's easy to say, but what does it really mean? A self-aware person understands his or her expected behavior on the team and actively manages his or her conduct accordingly. If a team is a collection of individuals, then it only makes sense that success or failure depends on each individual's self-awareness. The failure to apply this idea will almost certainly destroy an attempt at promoting accountability. Here are a few questions to get you thinking both personally and about your team. As you read these questions, consider how these individual behaviors can undermine your efforts to build a safety culture.

- **When issues arise, do you calmly address them, or do you go on the attack?** You become a bully, especially during difficult times, and you deflect everyone's focus from the issue at hand to fending off your attack.

- **Do you act one way around the leadership team and then in a less desirable way when with your peers?** You are enthusiastic and willing to support a procedure when you're in front of management, but turn around and have a negative attitude about it with your peers or team.

- **Do you conduct the "meeting after the meeting"?** In the meeting room, you appear appropriately aligned. You either do not speak up, or you vocally support the outcome. Then, after the meeting, you let everyone know what a stupid action plan was developed. You pit people against each other to promote unhealthy conflict, thinking that this wedge might somehow benefit you.

- **Are you overly dramatic?** Everything is a major production. You let everyone know how a company decision creates such a burden on you.

- **Do you prefer excuses to solutions?** You yield ownership for the task at hand and blame everyone else for why it is not proceeding as desired.

All of these examples have something in common. There is no policy or SOP that can fix them. Accountability is a function of how you choose to show up. Company executives are as prone to not being self-aware as anyone else in the company.

What Can You Do to Encourage Greater Organizational Accountability for Safety?

When something goes wrong, management's knee-jerk response must focus on these basic questions: What happened? What went wrong? Who or what directly caused the problem? That narrow inquiry leaves out the critical and often bigger question: *What are the underlying systemic processes or failures that directly caused or contributed to the problem?*

This is the step where you can fully let go of blame and establish a just and fair workplace environment. Demonstrate your willingness to dive into this second-tier inquiry with most problems and issues that undermine your company's success. Show your openness and receptivity to making changes at the top to support better performance with fewer mistakes on the front lines.

Making this change will go a long way toward cultivating the level playing field you need to build and sustain a vibrant culture.

What Can You Do to Encourage Greater Peer-to-Peer Accountability?

Getting employees to hold one another accountable can be challenging. For many employees it means stepping out of their comfort zone. Why are peers so reluctant to hold one another accountable? First, many of us were brought up in the outdated parent-child management structure. We fall victim to the old thinking that only managers should hold the rest of the team accountable. Second, it just doesn't come naturally for many people, including leaders. We all have a need to be liked. When we hold a fellow employee accountable, his or her reaction may be poor. People worry about being ostracized.

Here's how leaders can help. Remind employees that just as management is no longer playing the blame game, they need to cease that practice, too. Urge them to adopt the mindset that when something goes wrong they can choose to stand up and take responsibility for their part in the problem. While this may be uncomfortable at first, doing so will gain them greater respect from everyone on the team for their honesty and transparency. They will be modeling behavior for others to emulate.

Employees build trust with team members by speaking up. This is especially true when they acknowledge or validate something another teammate does well. Underscore your company value of teamwork. Acting on behalf of the team includes respectfully speaking up when a team member appears to be contributing to a problem or is acting inappropriately. When teammates consistently provide feedback, fellow team members will be more receptive when a peer points out a negative issue. Make sure that employees know that you are doing them a favor by helping correct the problem before it escalates further.

Help your employees recognize the downside of standing idly by. Watching a fellow employee drown could have consequences for the team, for the company, for customers, and possibly even for their own career. This is not about a popularity contest. It is about running (and being part of) a winning organization.

Holding people accountable is an acquired skill. Coach your team on how to do this. We like to follow the rule of being hard on the issue and soft on the people when an innocent mistake is made. Try not to make it an attack, and don't assume bad motives.

What if the employee that a peer is trying to hold accountable reacts poorly and says, "You're not my manager. Mind your own business!"? That is behavior we simply cannot accept. That employee needs to be coached, and if the employee refuses coaching, he or she is not likely to survive in a healthy safety culture.

CHAPTER 5:

Beyond Compliance: Safety and Regulatory Compliance Are Not the Same

Disconnect the words *safety* and *compliance*. They're not the same. Take the traditional safety model and break it into three parts as shown at the end of this chapter. The first part is incident and claims management. Anyone operating in any sort of a safety-sensitive business or advising clients who are in a safety-sensitive business must be proficient in this area should an accident happen.

We have to know what we're doing in the area of claims management. However, do we really want to become professional claims managers? Do we really want to be good at picking up the mess?

The second part of the safety model is regulatory compliance. That's part of staying in business. We can argue whether some regulations are good or bad, but we follow them because that's key to staying in business and it's the nonnegotiable right action to take.

The third part is where the real safety dividends exist—creating clear processes and managing behavior. What are you doing or what could you do to manage safety behavior? Here are a few ideas:

- **Ensure your employees report a near miss without fear of retribution.** This will allow you to diagnose and prevent near misses so that an actual accident does not occur in the future.

- **Get out on the floor.** Create a system of field-behavior observations to ensure employees are following processes.

- **Bring your front lines inside.** They have the best idea of where the risks lie and, if engaged, will be your greatest source of information. Lecture less and listen more.

- **Ensure an ongoing system of process audits exists.** Be your own worst critic to find flaws in the system and locate areas for improvement.

- **Promote a culture of accountability.** While we have hit this topic hard in this book, it all comes down to accountability. Every employee should adopt a mindset of prevention and should be personally accountable for making this happen both individually and peer to peer.

- **Do not compromise your preventive maintenance program (PM).** Ensure that your PM is disciplined and occurs on agreed intervals. We have seen too many situations where a PM is delayed because, "We are too busy." Nonsense! Saying that we are too busy to PM our equipment is the same as saying we are too busy to be safe.

- **Implement a new employee onboarding process that instills preventative behaviors from day one.** Just because a new hire knows how to execute a given job function does not mean that he or she knows how to do this in your organization and in line with your values.

We started the list for you. Now, what would you add to institutionalize prevention-based behaviors in your business?

SAFETY IS A STRATEGIC CHOICE

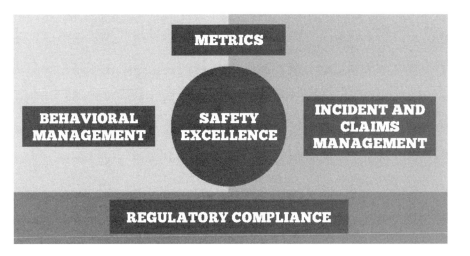

*Do not use "safety and compliance" in the same breath. Both are important but vastly different.
Safety is about prevention and behavior management.*

CHAPTER 6:

Safety Dysfunction: Good Can Be Bad

Carelessness and overconfidence are usually more dangerous than deliberately accepted risks.
—Wilbur Wright

Safety can be an unforgiving domain that grants no waivers. There is no credit for how good you were in the past. It doesn't care what you did last year, last month, last week, yesterday, or even one minute ago. Safety cares only about right now. It demands your full attention every second.

Safety is unfair. Think about it—if you live to be eighty years old, you will experience over 2.5 billion seconds of life. However, three seconds of distraction or poor decision-making is all it takes to dramatically alter or destroy the rest. Now *that* is unfair.

What makes it worse is that you don't get to choose the time of reckoning when a failure may occur. Catastrophic failure may sit dormant on the shelf for a long time and then strike when least expected. Safety risks may not always be where you think they are.

Safety Success in the Past Doesn't Guarantee Safety Success in the Future

You can look through hundreds of transportation accident reports over the years and clearly see that even the most experienced, knowledgeable, and capable professionals are not immune to accidents. There are some recent dramatic examples, such as Asiana Airlines flight 214, which crashed on approach to runway 28L at San Francisco International

Airport in July 2013. As reported in the press and affirmed in the NTSB investigation, the airplane was crewed by three highly experienced, highly trained, and seemingly highly motivated pilots who were flying a state-of-the-art Boeing 777 airplane. As documented in the NTSB report, despite nearly thirty-five thousand combined hours of experience as pilots, the airplane dropped too low and too slow on approach. The main gear wheels and undercarriage struck the seawall prior to arrival at the runway threshold, causing severe damage and loss of control. The airframe was destroyed, 187 people were injured, and three people died. This is just one example. There are countless more we could quote to attest to the fact that people of high skill and practice have found themselves involved in a breach of safety in many industries.

So why does this happen?

Our thesis is that *good* can be *bad*. By that we mean that good performers, be they individuals, groups, or companies, must guard against a false sense of invulnerability. Put another way, good performance and an absence of accidents can promote complacency—satisfaction with one's accomplishments, accompanied by a lack of awareness of actual dangers or deficiencies.

The tendency to get complacent is not an uncommon trait in humans, but if allowed to establish itself, it can destroy a culture of safety. In our experience, complacency creep generally occurs silently and gradually. Someone once referred to it as the "walrus effect." A walrus isn't born ugly. It gets that way over time. That's how it is with complacency, too. If you're not paying attention, before you know it, you'll have an ugly cultural issue to deal with.

Sometimes Good Isn't Good Enough: The Clarion Call

Let's say your group has a good safety culture. Your company hasn't experienced any serious safety failures, injuries, or accidents so far. You are by all measures a good performer. Congratulations!

Don't get too comfortable, though. Ask yourself if your good performance is the result of a healthy culture, strength of leadership, team alignment, and good processes, or if the good safety is just pure luck. If you answer that it's all because of luck, you need to get serious about safety right now.

One characteristic that distinguishes good companies is the ability to have a balanced view of themselves. The leaders do not ignore the facts even if they are unpleasant. They recognize the need to be obsessed with continuous safety improvement. They also recognize that complacency creep is real.

Dysfunctional Creep Happens

In our seventy-plus combined years' experience in organizational trenches, we have encountered and overcome dysfunctional routines that challenged the care and feeding of a positive culture of safety. Below we offer twelve of the more dangerous routines, or challenges, that we have seen affront the building of good safety cultures. These are elements of "organizational cholesterol" that build over time. Unless recognized, diagnosed, and addressed, they will make a good safety culture sick.

Challenge 1: "That's right, we bad." This line was made famous in *Stir Crazy*, a 1980 movie with Richard Pryor and Gene Wilder. The two portray men who are framed and sent to jail. Far from tough, they chant, "That's right, we bad," as they walk into the jail cell, hoping to at least intimidate other inmates. While funny in the movie, it isn't funny in the corporate world. Believing that you are "bad" (i.e., "good") and acting with a swagger may be innocuous if you have the performance to back it up, but when you start to believe your own good news—that you are truly "bad," you are setting up failure. In his book *Darker Shades of Blue: The Rogue Pilot*, Dr. Tony Kern perhaps said it best: "A safety culture must be inspired and constantly nurtured to prevent that downward spiral into disaster."

Challenge 2: Declaring victory before getting to the finish line. You may think you are good, and you may be ahead of other groups or your competitors in your safety, productivity, or financial numbers. However, beware of premature declarations that you have won. You haven't. We see this happen all the time in athletics. A sprinter with arms raised in victory before the final tape, only to be eclipsed at the end by a surging runner; the running back spiking the ball for dramatic effect after a long run in a football game, before crossing the goal line; a basketball player celebrating with an on-court dance after making a go-ahead goal at the close of a game, only to look foolish when the opposing team throws a lucky half-court shot to win the game. Early celebrations of victory before a sporting event is over may be embarrassing in sports, but in business they can prove disastrous.

Challenge 3: Tolerating toxic people. Toxic people sabotage good social order and team alignment by robbing positive emotional and intellectual energy from the good people. T. S. Eliot wrote in *The Cocktail Party* that "Half the harm that is done in this world is due to people who want to feel important. . . . They are absorbed in the endless struggle to think well of themselves." These are the people in your organization with uncontrolled egos. They may be rude know-it-alls with condescending attitudes. They generally are chronic complainers—the passive-aggressive types who chip away at morale. Here are a few examples of specific toxic behaviors that must be rejected:

- **When the meeting ends, the treachery begins.**
  A Malayan proverb says, "Don't think there are no crocodiles because the water is calm." That applies in spades here. Suppose you have a cordial, apparently collaborative meeting where issues are raised and discussed and decisions are made. Everyone around the table nods and ostensibly agrees. You have a plan, right? Not if there is an agitator in the room. Despite seemingly offering support during the meeting, once the meeting ends, this person subverts established forums by storming outside with covert resistance to discredit and undermine the team.

- **Privileging blue bloods.** "Blue bloods" are people who believe that organizational longevity entitles them to exclusive privilege. We have seen this toxic quality manifest in behaviors that fit under several general statements or categories:

  o "*I have paid my dues.*" Someone did a good job last week, last month, or last year, so now he or she rationalizes that it is OK to let up. In effect, this person is saying, "I don't need to work as hard now." Contrast that to good companies where there is an atmosphere of teamwork and where people understand that dues must be paid every day if the team is to compete.

  o "*I have a lot of experience here.*" Experience alone is not a tangible commodity. A history of showing up at the workplace in itself doesn't merit special reverence. While experience may be important, unless it delivers better performance and enables higher skills, it is without value. In effect, people who say this are really saying, "I don't have to be part of the team. I don't need to justify my actions." Simply having experience should never trump hard work and execution.

o *"It's not my job."* Saying "It's not my job" is akin to saying "I don't care about the team. I care only about me." This attitude destroys team performance and can quickly turn a potentially coalesced team into a troubled collection of individuals. Good companies establish teams that demonstrate willingness to do whatever it takes to be successful, as long as their action isn't unethical or illegal. In fact, good people look for problems and intervene before being asked.

o *"You make the rest of us look bad."* Peer pressure can be a persuasive force, be it good or bad. Unfortunately, we have seen a great deal of bad peer pressure applied to stifle good performers. This manifestation seems to be one of human nature's most common qualities. Putting down high achievers begins as early as childhood. Think about the girl or boy in your school class who always had the answers, turned in completed assignments, and aced every test. Other children typically scorned and isolated these kids. Sadly, as adults, this trait remains fully entrenched and, in some instances, intensifies. A weak employee tries to glide and do only enough to get by. There is no desire to win, only the desire to not look bad in the shadow of a high performer. As a result, this person will pull out the stops to demean the high performers through gossip, sabotage, or ridicule. Albert Einstein nailed it when he said, "Great spirits have always encountered violent opposition from mediocre minds."

- **Fostering a culture of denial.** This is where new, creative, and original ideas are executed. These people are professional cynics and delight in saying no. Their refrain is familiar: "It's too expensive," or "You don't understand the way things are done here," or "We've tried things like this before, and it didn't work." They ensure negative cogency permeates any team, and they seem to take pride in stifling originality. The "no" people poison group resourcefulness and eradicate team optimism.

- **Allowing chaos and complexity to rule.** Confucius is supposed to have said, "Life is really simple, but we insist on making it complicated." Some people thrive on chaos. They manage to complicate even basic initiatives with overanalyzing and complex decision-making matrixes that require multiple approvals. Everybody has to say yes, but anybody can say no. They never deliver because there is a loss of focus on doing the basics well. These people muddle efficient practices and frustrate team progress.

- **Tolerating gossip crusaders.** Gossip crusaders have one singular mission: to spread rumors and discontent. These people thrive on drama and disruption. They have few priorities except to talk about other people. In turn, they waste time better spent on positive tasks for the customer, while actively diminishing the dignity of coworkers. We have heard people say that gossip is human nature and that it does little real harm. We disagree. Gossip is like a lit match. On the surface, it is just a tiny flame that seems harmless. However, left unattended in the wrong place, that tiny flame can burn down a majestic forest. Good leaders don't allow a culture of gossip to prevail.

- **Tolerating glory keepers.** Nothing important is ever accomplished alone. Even if a star player did most of the work, good and sustained results inevitably require a team effort. People who say, "It was all my idea," or "I made it happen," are, in effect, saying, "I am more important than everyone else on the team." This attitude causes other members to harbor resentment, which leads to loss of team amiability and lessened productivity.

- **Tolerating under-the-bus-they-go characters.** Along with glory keepers, these characters are masters at avoiding accountability. No matter what has happened, it's always someone else's fault. The only time these people want to accept responsibility is when a positive outcome brings credit. In good companies, teams have a view that win, lose, or draw, they are all in this together.

Challenge 4: "It Won't Happen to Me" (IWHTM) syndrome. Some people believe they are bulletproof. If you have someone with the IWHTM syndrome, you have someone who will likely be reckless and out of control. This attitude leads to certain trouble, especially in high-consequence environments. Files are full of accident investigations where someone caused bad results because they believed IWHTM.

Challenge 5: Losing respect for standard operating procedures (SOPs). In high-consequence activities, people must follow standard procedures, rules, and practices. Freelancing and just winging it are highly risky. One of the most common examples of this phenomenon may be the notion of selective compliance. Here, people choose which rules and procedures to obey and which to ignore. We live in a world of rules, and we elect people to make more rules. However, the hard truth is that if you want a culture of total safety, there must be respect for all rules. If a rule doesn't make sense, eliminate it. Why don't people follow SOPs? We think there are five main reasons:

1. The organization may not have adequate SOPs.

2. There is poor organizational commitment to SOP adherence, so individuals let up.

3. There is intentional disregard of SOPs.

4. The SOPs lack credibility and therefore are ignored.

5. The organization has not adequately communicated the SOPs in a way in which they are understood at all levels of the company.

Challenge 6: Normalization of deviance. This is when people within an organization become accustomed to shortcuts and deviant behaviors in the conduct of their work. Over time, with no consequence for the deviations, the shortcuts become the norm. People involved inside the organization fail to recognize the danger of the new normal. There has been much written on this topic, but the theory gained prominence as a result of Diane Vaughan's 1996 book *The* Challenger *Launch Decision* in which she details how the ethics of the normalization of deviance at NASA resulted in a design flaw in certain performance capabilities involving joint seals on the solid rocket booster. This defect resulted in failure shortly after launch, with the subsequent loss of the *Challenger* space shuttle and its crew on January 28, 1986. Vaughan pointed out how "evidence initially interpreted as a deviation from expected performance was reinterpreted as within the bounds of acceptable risk."

Probably the most obvious current-day example of normalization of deviance that we can think of is the use of personal electronic devices (PEDs) while operating a vehicle. Virtually everyone we know admits that using PEDs while driving is dangerous. Yet, even with laws in many jurisdictions prohibiting such use behind the wheel, people still do it. It has become the "norm."

Challenge 7: Overcomplicating things. "When you hear hoof beats, think horses, not zebras." We like that aphorism because it points out the folly of confusing even simple concepts. Some people have a penchant to obfuscate everything. They put too much emphasis on process and little on outcomes and content. There is a flurry of activity, but little substance results. In our experience, safety is all about executing the fundamentals. If you do the basics well, everything else will normally follow. No need to try a triple-reverse pirouette off the high dive to get wet. Just jump into the water.

Challenge 8: Getting lost in the numbers. In 1963, William Bruce Cameron wrote, "Not everything that can be counted counts, and not everything that counts can be counted," in his work *Informal Sociology: A Casual Introduction to Sociological Thinking*. The lesson here is that you must measure more than outcomes. Measures should encompass process and execution, too. Measuring just outcomes is like trying to win a game by looking only at the scoreboard. If you execute the basics on the field, the score will follow. Also, ensure the metrics used are clear, direct, and easy for everyone in the organization to understand. Then, be patient. When you undertake a safety culture renovation, your safety numbers may actually get worse before they get better due to a more open, trusting culture. The uptick likely means that you are getting better information and a more accurate view of the real underlying risk issues as people learn to trust the process.

Challenge 9: Trying to perfume the pig. A pig is a pig, even if you try to disguise it with perfume. So it is in some companies. Managers try to disguise problems through what we call "happy talk." These are people who extend effort to avoid candid conversations. In the process, they redefine "good" to avoid the truth. Constructive conflict is an important and essential part of organizational life. Trying to put perfume on a problem won't make it go away. It most likely just temporarily masks it. It is best to deal with it head on.

Our job as leaders is to promote fierce discussions around the topic of safety, yet too often we sugarcoat these discussions. "We reduced our accidents by 25 percent. Isn't that great?" Not really. It means we are "less bad" but still 75 percent away from zero. Now, we are not suggesting that you ignore positive signs of progress. The safety journey is often incremental, and progress is measured in inches. As you pause to recognize a milestone, celebrate quickly and then get back to work on the journey to excellence.

It's not hard to know why we avoid difficult conversations in so many meetings. They are uncomfortable. Perhaps we don't want to offend others in the room. Perhaps we view the conversation as being "not my responsibility." Our role is not to worry about hurt feelings or sensitive egos. Our role is to ensure that we are confronting safety challenges through fact-based, frank conversations about becoming better tomorrow than today. Team members who are satisfied with being "less bad" ultimately will undermine your journey to a world-class safety culture.

Challenge 10: "This too shall pass." With this challenge, some people in the trenches fail to commit to the vision. They think if they hunker down, the safety focus will fade. Unfortunately, this behavior is common in some companies because in past plans management lost interest and continually pivoted from one initiative to another. At the outset, make your opening moves so compelling that there is no doubt that the current status quo is unacceptable. Then, enforce the culture every day, even when it is hard to do. Consistency and resolve are central tenets to sustain a positive culture.

Challenge 11: Allowing regulators to drive safety culture. The people in the organization must define and own the culture. When regulators and politicians dictate the structure of your safety programs, there is by design a low probability that you will instill a vigorous and comprehensive safety culture. Regulations provide only the minimums to get by. You want to do much more than that.

Challenge 12: Forgetting who has the power in your organization. Who would you say is the most powerful person in your company? It is likely that you will immediately respond "the CEO," or "the president." In our view, the most powerful people are the ones who have day-to-day domain over resources and who are the points of direct contact with the customer. To be sure, the CEO, president, and senior managers have authority. However, do they really have the power? Recognizing the difference between power and authority is an important attribute of great leaders and great companies. Power resides in the front line. Few CEOs, presidents, and senior managers can do the tasks necessary to meet customer expectations. Besides, your front line knows where real risks lie. They are the subject-matter experts. They have the answers.

"Do. Or do not. There is no try."—Yoda
Life is dynamic. So is business. The business battlefield is always evolving. You will either get better and become one of the great, legendary companies, or get worse and allow dysfunction to creep into the culture. As Yoda says in *Star Wars: Episode V*, "Do. Or do not. There is no try." Just trying to keep up with change will reserve your place as an "also ran" in the future competitive marketplace. Alan Kay said, "The best way to predict the future is to create it." Thus, we must ask several questions: What is the personality of your culture? Are you immune to dysfunctional challenges like the ones we just reviewed? Are you ready to lead your team in creating and sustaining a culture of positive safety, or are you going along for the ride?

We have learned over the years that an organization will "talk" to you. It may speak through a series of close calls in safety, or it may speak through the occurrence of a minor accident. It could appear in the form of high turnover in the ranks or, perhaps, growing discipline problems. It might even be your gut as a seasoned executive telling you that something is not quite right. All these can be indicators that dysfunction and discontent may be sneaking into your organizational blood flow. Whatever it is saying, you need to be tuned in, listen, and take action.

One way to ensure management hears what is going on is to conduct regular "start-stop-keep" discussions with the front line. In this exercise, ask your people these questions: What aren't we doing that we need to start? What are we doing that we need to stop? What are we doing that we need to keep doing? You would be surprised how effective this exercise is in helping you monitor the group. It also enables your front line to feel included and feel that they have impact. You benefit by possibly getting some new ideas on how to better accomplish the mission while eliminating non-value-adding activities.

A Lifelong Burden

Allowing safety dysfunctions to occur on your watch may take a lifelong toll on you personally. For example, when NASA rocket engineer Bob Ebeling passed away in March 2016, the Associated Press reported:

> "Bob Ebeling spent three decades filled with guilt over not stopping the explosion of the space shuttle *Challenger* . . . Ebeling warned his boss the morning before the launch of the dangers that could face the *Challenger* if it was sent into space that day . . . [Ebeling] watched live video of the *Challenger* clearing the launch pad on January 28 [1986]. [He was heard to say,] "It's not over." About twenty second later, the shuttle exploded."

While Mr. Ebeling took every possible action to prevent the fatal launch, it was not enough. We can all learn tremendous lessons from the crushing burden that Mr. Ebeling carried with him for three decades. You must speak as loud as possible until you are heard. If you are not heard after reasonable effort, decide whether or not you have a duty to the public that is greater than your duty to the company. Also, consider whether you should take your talents elsewhere. Finally, ensure each team member understands that ignoring safety dysfunctions may create a personal, crushing, lifelong burden.

PART II:

How to Build a World-Class Safety Culture

CHAPTER 7:

A Case Study

There is nothing more difficult to take in hand, more perilous to conduct, or more uncertain in its success, because the innovator has for enemies all those who have done well under the old conditions, and lukewarm defenders in those who may do well under the new.
—Niccolò Machiavelli

Convincing people to change is not an easy task, especially when people are comfortable in their situations. We want to highlight how we were able to lead teams in the transformation of the safety culture of a major company as an illustration. In late 2000, Jim assumed command of the safety program in this company; the program was highly decentralized, marginalized, and misunderstood. Brand new in the role, we didn't fully appreciate the scope of the challenge. The CEO was recently appointed to the company, too.

While Jim and his team were new, the existing field management cadre was well established. Most were veterans of the industry with years of experience in the craft and highly skeptical of anyone from outside the industry. The negative inertia was palpable. The incumbent culture rejected the advice, opinions and expertise offered by anyone they perceived to be an outsider. The management was awash in overconfidence that was unjustified given the performance that we soon uncovered.

Our Starting Point: What We Inherited
Within a month of arrival in the new role, the CEO asked us

what the company's safety performance numbers were for the year. In most companies, especially big companies, this is an entirely reasonable question. However, in our situation with no real central metrics, it turned out to be a major research effort. We had to pretty much go location by location, as well as deep-dive insurance claims and settlement numbers. When all was said and done, we were stunned at the results. For the calendar year 2000, we found:

- fifty-nine fatalities reported in company operations (fifteen on-duty employees and forty-four non-employees);

- an Occupational Safety and Health Administration (OSHA) employee recordable injury rate at twenty-one-plus (the US norm per OSHA for this industry was around five in 2000);

- about 12,500 workers' compensation claims filed;

- about $150 million-plus spent on workers' compensation costs (which did not include corollary or indirect costs, such as lost productivity and revenue, hiring replacements, customer dissatisfaction, and rework);

- about twenty-three thousand property damage claims submitted for company equipment or customer property;

- no system metrics, no common processes, and no enterprise focus on total company impact; and

- over three hundred safety managers on staff.

Most companies would sound the panic claxon with these results, declaring a major crisis. Just consider the workers' comp cost alone—$150 million a year correlates to almost $411,000 a day in the hole 365 days a year. How many customer interactions did it take just to break even each day before profits? Wouldn't that fact alone result in major action? But there was no alarm. In fact, in early 2001 we commissioned a company-wide independent assessment conducted by a credible outside consulting firm. The results of that assessment were astonishing. The vast majority of company managers rated themselves as A to A-minus regarding their self-evaluated safety leadership effectiveness.

Some might also wonder how these high casualty numbers could happen with over three hundred safety people assigned throughout the field organization. What were they doing while all this was happening? We'll address that issue in the coming paragraphs.

Not surprisingly, once informed of the results, the CEO's question was "How are we going to fix this?"

Our Flight Plan: How We Addressed the Culture
We believe that major transformational change requires a plan. This kind of change will not naturally evolve. Here, we present the highlights of our plan to address the culture.

Conduct gap analysis. First, we needed to conduct a comprehensive gap analysis to identify what was driving the dismal safety performance. Here are some of the major gaps we identified:

- **Delegated safety leadership.** Operating management believed that they were too important to get involved in the details.

- **Isolated safety responsibility.** The general mindset was that safety belonged only to the safety manager.

- **Blame culture.** Management accepted no responsibility for safety failures. Blame was the name of the game, and usually the person at the end of the line was nailed.

- **Reactive versus preventative focus.** It is a sorry state when one of your core competencies is picking up wrecks and carrying injured employees to the hospital. That was the reality.

- **Flying blind: no common metrics.** There was no enterprise IT capacity in the company given the wide disparity in data collection and management capabilities of the various roll ups. That resulted in deviating safety metrics that lacked both consistency and standardization.

- **No respect for procedural compliance.** The incumbent culture did not revere standardized procedures. There was a wholesale "à la carte" culture where local management could pick and choose which rules and procedures they did or did not follow.

- **No Safety Management System (SMS) ethic.** There was no SMS focus. In fact, the concept of SMS and the four pillars of program governance were totally foreign to the majority of people, including the hundreds of assigned field safety managers.

- **No enterprise view.** This was a huge company with enormous potential franchise power. Field locations and regions were so highly siloed that they didn't know how their individual performance impacted the mother company.

- **Low expectations: "Things happen."** Management believed that they were victims of circumstance. We heard it a thousand times if we heard it once, to the effect of "We can't control what goes on out there," "people do dumb things," and "there are going to be injuries and wrecks." In effect, management gave themselves a pass.

- **No sense of urgency.** It was surprising that even with the high casualty numbers, costs, and turmoil, there was no sense of urgency about getting ahold of safety performance. The attitude was "I'm OK, you're OK, now let's go have lunch."

- **Happy talk.** For an operating company from an industry with much machismo, there was minimal candid conversation around the reality of the performance. The failure to confront poor performers, both individually and collectively, enabled crummy results. Those crummy results then became the norm.

What made changing behaviors a more formidable challenge was the fact that managers were very comfortable. By virtue of a strong franchise, the company was making money, salaries were good, and bonuses were paid. Safety was really not on the daily radar due in large measure to an absence of good data. People really didn't know how bad it was. The safety information that was provided was in the form of cold statistics—numbers on paper devoid of emotion or meaning. Making a case for change in a culture where people are benefitting from the status quo compounds the effort significantly.

Start "ab initio." There is lore from ancient Greece that at one time the Athenians, alarmed at the internal decay of their Republic, asked Demosthenes what to do. His reply: "Do not do what you are doing now." With information established through the gap analysis, it was clear at this point that we needed to start *"ab initio"* (from the beginning). There was little good to be salvaged from the sitting programs given the record of fatalities, injuries, high costs, poor morale, damaged social reputation in communities, major property damage, bad asset utilization, customer service failures, and lack of management accountability. We could no longer continue to do what we were doing. It was entirely obvious that we needed to find a much more powerful engine to drive the safety culture going forward.

Make it personal. We made safety personal. No longer did we talk only in terms of numbers. We also talked about the people involved and their families and how they were impacted. We took safety from the abstract and attached real humans to the equation. This was highly effective in overcoming the filters. Try this experiment next time you pick up your local newspaper: turn to the obituary page and pick out one or two. As you read through the details, the reality sets in that these were people, just like you. They had dreams, they had lives, they had families. No longer are they just statistics. They are real. Making it real by putting the human with the statistic is a very effective way to overcome safety malaise. In addition to the emotional pull, you also need to give people a stake in safety success. We tied bonus, salary, and promotions to safety performance, as well as appealing to the good side of people. To be sure, you must ensure your systems don't tolerate manipulation just to meet the numbers, but there must be linkage. Ultimately, people who could not lead their teams safely and who did not buy into the vision had to go.

Kill the sacred cows. We declared that we had embarked on a new journey—one on which the old "sacred cows" from the past could not go. We identified those cows and executed them. One of the sacred cows was that safety belonged to the safety manager. Wrong. In an operating company, safety belongs to operating management. The safety manager is a coach and teacher. Another sacred cow was the victim mentality that was rooted in the culture, that is, "Poor us, we work in a dangerous environment. Accidents will happen," thereby giving themselves a pass on being accountable for outcomes.

Identify the organizational role. We introduced the concept of organizational causes for safety failures. That means the organization has a role, usually a huge role, regarding fault when something goes wrong. Some examples include employees developing work-arounds instead of following procedures, the organization not learning from prior events and precursors, senior management giving only lip service to safety, management not knowing what is driving safety performance, and the organization using incorrect metrics to gauge safety. This company was excellent at pointing fingers and assessing blame—usually targeting the person at the point where the problem occurred. They would fire or discipline the offender, then move on with no focus on determining root causes and how to prevent the problem in the future.

Align with the "North Star" themes. This was our clarion call. We knew it was critical to quickly establish alignment around a durable go-forward doctrine—the rules of the game that defined how we were going to drive performance going forward. The first group we had to enlist was the senior team, followed by the general management team, including the field safety managers. We recognized that an organization, to paraphrase Ralph Waldo Emerson, is the lengthened shadow of its senior team. When the senior team is not aligned, the organization cannot be aligned. Without alignment, performance suffers. Thus, we first targeted the senior management, and these twelve principles were nonnegotiable. The CEO had to own the new doctrine. He made it clear from the outset that there was no equivocation on these behavioral standards. They were, in substance, our "North Stars" on which the whole company had to focus to be aligned properly.

- **Safety has to be a core value, not just a priority.** Priorities change every day. Values do not.

- **There must be a leadership obsession with continuous improvement every day—a "chronic unease" with the status quo.** "Chronic unease" is a term we first heard used by Dr. James Reason. Without this, you risk creeping complacency that invades processes.

- **Zero is the only acceptable goal.** For most aspects of business, 99.9 percent is a pretty compelling standard. Not safety. Zero safety failures is the only goal that is satisfactory.

- **Safety is about you.** It isn't just statistics. It is families and friends. Safety is much more than a group of numbers on a page.

- **Managers have to engage.** This can't be delegated. Safety leadership is a core responsibility of management.

- **Measurement of performance is critical.** Measure what drives performance, not just the accident rate. The accident rate is the outcome of behaviors, so measure proactive activities like safety meetings, supervisory and peer observations, individual one-on-one discussions, and cultural surveys.

- **It is a low-cost solution.** No big capital is needed. A culture of positive safety is based on engaging people around a vision and each person accepting accountability for results. It doesn't require much capital.

- **This can be done with little organizational turmoil.** In a poor safety culture, you can't fire everybody and start over. You have to make it work with the incumbent team. This is about providing a compelling case for change and bringing people to a new way of thinking and acting, of holding themselves and others accountable for safety. The few who don't buy in need to find somewhere else to work.

- **The majority of casualties are caused by at-risk behavior, not a pure failure in facilities or equipment.** Rather than examining the conditions of the accident, it is more useful to consider the behavior associated with it.

- **Rules, laws, regulations, and proscriptions alone do not prevent accidents.** It takes a culture where every individual worker buys into safety. Safety is about people taking responsibility for their behavior and that of their peers.

- **Focus on the basics.** Great safety is about paying attention to detail and solidly executing the basics.

- **"Just culture" is the cornerstone for great safety. Great safety is the cornerstone for best-in-class operations.** People align with management's vision and engage at a much higher level when they feel valued and appreciated. Many studies have shown that when people feel included and that they are making a difference, they will give much higher differential effort to help the group succeed. That means higher productivity, a better customer experience, better resource utilization and care, and less waste.

Remember your middle management. Too many times, senior management forgets to take their frontline and mid-level managers with them when implementing new strategies. Unless you have your frontline managers on board, your strategy will never work. Your mid-level people scuttle or advance any senior management plan. These people are the intimate interface with employees on all matters. As you might expect, when we first launched, there was the usual pushback. Frazzled middle managers thought the new program would mean more work for them. Anyone who has spent time in mid-management roles can easily understand this reasoning. Someone once said that for most people at this level, life is like a fire hydrant: spending all day putting out fires and standing ground against the big dogs.

Establish pride in the craft. For some of the employees, youthful dreams and once-big plans had fizzled. Life for some had evolved into a colorless routine of low expectations. We had people who were drifting through their jobs with quiet submission, engaged in work too small for their spirits. One of the great blessings about being in a leadership role, however, is the ability to change this by providing people a higher calling in their work. So it was in the turnaround. Our people needed to feel like their daily toil was making a contribution to society. This is a basic human need, whether you are working in the corner office or as a common laborer. You need to feel like what you're doing is meaningful. We started to talk to our frontline people about the significance of their work in keeping good social order. We bought new uniforms for the front line, all standardized with proper branding and logos. We ordered logoed flags for facilities. We invested in new trucks and painted the names of drivers on the door (a practice used in fighter aviation). All this elevated the way our employees viewed themselves and the company. It was a big deal.

Reallocate the field safety staff. We mentioned there

were over three hundred field safety managers on staff in 2000. Despite their presence, safety was not good, as noted. One reason, we discovered, was that field safety people were generally viewed as clerks. They collected tolls, managed claims, and maintained federal forms. Since we believe that safety is the responsibility of operating management rather than a safety manager, we eliminated most of the field safety jobs over five years and reassigned them into front-line operating roles after gaining their alignment with the vision. That enabled migration of the message down into the bowels of the organization, accelerating change.

We cannot emphasize loudly enough that "safety silos" must be torn down. Safety is not a department. It is a way of life. In a healthy safety culture, safety excellence is everyone's responsibility. It should be a warning sign if safety problems are thrust upon your safety department and everyone else walks away. Having a safety department in and of itself cannot raise the bar on safety. Your safety department can coach, train, mentor, and create account-ability. They are your subject-matter experts. That said, only people with their hands on the levers can execute upon safety. These are your operators, managers, and frontline employees. Your system of bonuses and rewards must take into account safety performance at the operational level. These employees are the individuals who are responsible for safe outcomes. Decoupling the safety and operations departments only blurs accountability and creates orga-nizational confusion. Safety in its truest form is all about collaboration among individuals in your organization with diverse functional backgrounds.

Debunk the safety-or-productivity dichotomy. "Safety or productivity—which one do you want?" We have heard it our entire careers from the unenlightened: "You can't be safe and be productive at the same time, so what do you want: to get the job done, or for us to be safe?" This is a fallacy. If you want to have a messed-up operation, just experience unplanned down time from a bad injury or equipment damage. See what being unsafe does to your operation, your budget, your customer service, your reputation in the community, and your total costs. Best-in-class leaders and best-in-class companies know that safety is the cornerstone of great operations.

Burn the ships. Upon arrival in the New World in 1519, Cortés called his sailors to the shore, and while they watched, he summarily burned the ships to make clear to his sailors that there was no retreat and no going back. In effect, he was saying, "We're in a new world, and we have to make this work." We can learn several lessons from Cortés and his strategy that correlate to transforming a safety culture today:

- **It is an all-or-nothing mentality.** When Cortés scuttled his ships, he left no doubt that he was committed. It is the same in transformational change. You have to show with actions that the status quo is no longer acceptable.

- **Actions speak volumes.** We all have been in organizations where there is much talk about initiatives and priorities. Cortés let his actions speak, and there was little doubt to his people that he was serious. Like Cortés, you must take a stand and prove through actions that you are serious about change. People will believe and do what they see their managers do, not always what they hear them say. When Jim and team implemented the new discipline policy at CSX, they in effect "burned the ships" by giving everyone in the system a new start. The old progressive discipline records were ceremoniously "burned" so that everyone knew that it was a new day. There was no going back.

- **Think outside the box.** Cortés was a creative guy. Burning his ships in front of his men made a big impression and was something they most certainly didn't expect. So it is when you attempt to drive change. Dare to be different and shake things up. One of the first steps we took to disrupt the existing state of affairs was to stop comparing our performance to others in our industry, as was the standard for years. Instead, we picked groups with a certain mystique as world-class achievers as our yardstick, such as military fighter aviation and NASA.

- **Confidence is crucial.** Cortés was confident and let it show. As a result, his troops believed they would be successful. We had to demonstrate that this was the real deal and that we knew it would work.

Our Flight Plan: How We Transformed the Culture

As we have alluded, moving culture in a new direction will not happen by chance. You have to have a plan. Our plan has nine specific steps founded upon John P. Kotter's change management process outlined in his 1996 book *Leading Change*, combined with methodologies that have worked for us in driving change in large, complex, and often-reluctant organizations.

1. **Appoint a champion.** Here is your driving force. This is a fearless, passionate, and credible promoter to energize and direct the day-to-day execution. This is not the CEO, although the CEO must be seen as the sponsor and must engage

and be readily visible in the journey. The champion should be someone in a senior role with the charisma and tenacity to keep the inertia and not allow naysayers to derail the journey.

2. **Incite emotion.** The journey has to have emotion and energy. Kotter calls it "a sense of urgency." There must be a compelling reason for everyone in the organization to buy in to the program. The employees must understand why you are doing this and why it benefits them as individuals.

3. **Establish vision.** Business-leadership guru Jack Welch nailed it in a *Harvard Business Review* article called "Speed, Simplicity, Self-Confidence: An Interview with Jack Welch." In that article, Welch said, "Good business leaders create a vision, articulate the vision, passionately own the vision, and relentlessly drive it to completion." The safety vision has to be simple, direct, applicable, and understood by each individual. Our vision during this rebuild was, "We are going to zero." Everyone understood that they had to do their part to achieve the vision.

4. **Promote advocacy.** This is where the magic happens. Kotter calls this a "guiding coalition." In substance, you find a diverse, credible group of people in the organization, gain their buy-in first, and then ordain them as ambassadors. As they circulate in the organizational trenches, they "preach the gospel," and, because they are credible, others take note.

5. **Launch consistent communications and branding.** This is your vehicle to wrap the message and keep it front and center. The importance of

doing this step right cannot be overstated. People want to belong to something that's really neat, and branding and communications create the mystique.

6. **Create the process.** Establish procedures, processes, and tactics that reinforce the strategy. These are the tools that bring the vision to reality and enable you to operationalize your values.

7. **Implement measures.** Metrics must reflect the right outcomes. They must be simple and easily understood by everyone in the organization so that people know how their performance impacts the numbers. Measurement should focus more on process and less on outcomes. It is about how you play the game—what people are doing to drive the outcomes. Focusing on process and getting it right will put good numbers on the scoreboard.

8. **Anchor the culture.** To sustain and keep momentum, you must anchor the new culture by rewarding the right behaviors and celebrating early successes to overcome the naysayers trying to claim defeat at every setback. We call these "skid marks" that give everyone a clear notion of what is expected and what is rewarded in the new culture.

9. **Start over.** Admiral Hyman G. Rickover said, "Good ideas are not adopted automatically. They must be driven into practice with courageous patience. Once implemented they can be easily overturned or subverted through apathy or lack of follow-up . . . a continuous effort is required." No truer words were ever spoken about the effort it takes to sustain programs involving people in pursuit of opera-

tional excellence. In our experience, about every three years the program needs a rebooting and recharging of the entire process. Like any human-based program, there is a tendency for complacency creep, especially as people get accustomed over time to the new normal.

The Results

In five years, our casualty experience had improved by about 75 percent. The culture took root, and people in the organization internalized the processes and assumed responsibility for execution, holding themselves and their coworkers accountable. At first there was wide belief in the management group that pushing for "zero" casualties was wholly unreasonable. By the end of year five, about 60 percent of the operating locations had achieved the goal. People were believers. Credit goes to senior management for admitting the need to improve, personally engaging in the journey, and committing time and resources to drive improvement.

At the start of the implementation, the actuarial injury costs forecast for the year were approximately $150 million. Five years later, the actuarial injury costs forecast for the year were approximately $75 million. These are not company numbers but those provided by the contracted insurance actuaries. Insurance actuaries and insurance executives consistently told us that they had never seen a company show such a dramatic reduction in such a short period of time.

Early in the transformation, over one thousand employees were out of work due to an on-duty injury. Five years later, this number was reduced to less than one hundred. In addition, five hundred employees were terminated the first year due to actions that resulted in an on-duty injury, necessitating hiring, training, and integrating replacement employees. Five years later, less than fifty employees were terminated for actions that resulted in an on-duty injury.

Due to the success of the program, the deductible levels for insurance were increased substantially—from $1 million to $5 million in compensation and from $100,000 to $10 million in liability. This change saved millions of dollars in insurance costs and allowed us to manage claims with less involvement from the insurance company.

Managing Casualties until You Get to Zero: What Worked for Us

As we stated, the goal is zero casualties. However, until you get to zero, there needs to be an aggressive and well-managed post-injury process. Again, leadership is key to successful management of injury follow-up when one occurs. In our successful program, we established five key management oversight activities:

1. **Recognize the financial impact of safety failures.** We provided field operating site management with instant knowledge of the financial impact of all injuries and accidents on their Profit and Loss (P&L) statement in several ways:

   - Allocating the cost of each injury or accident to the monthly P&L, at the lowest level possible

   - Providing cost data in a usable format for comparison to other site operating costs (e.g., cost per man-hour for workers' compensation and cost per productive hour for accidents)

2. **Manage transitional returns to work.** We established a robust return-to-work program for all injured workers. Within that, we developed meaningful transitional assignments with constant follow-up by professionals working with local

management. We implemented this with several strategies:

- The longer an employee is off from injury, the more cost is normally incurred by the company. Instead of hiding this cost by corporate paying the tab, we allocated a daily fee to the local site operation for every day the injured employee was not in a return-to-duty transitional assignment. This put the financial pain where it needed to be to motivate local management to work with injured employees to get them back to work.

- We used assigned and dedicated professional occupational health counselors to work with local management to develop transitional jobs and monitor performance until the employee's full return to work. The counselors were also good independent auditors to limit potential gamesmanship in the site administration of the programs and cost allocations.

3. **Provide aggressive claims and legal management.** We identified the top 10 percent of claims that represented 80 percent of total company costs and targeted management focus.

- We set clear goals for claim adjusters to reduce open claim inventory and audit to these goals at least quarterly. We used dedicated adjusters with jurisdiction across multiple states, and it was very effective in bringing order and accountability to claims oversight.

- We selected one law firm by state (versus the incumbent process where dozens of firms were used) to manage claims, and we educated them on our programs. We then required aggressive action from them to move cases to conclusion. This gave us much more control over outside law firm activities.

4. **Educate the actuaries.** Independent actuaries effectively determine the financial success of your safety and cost reduction programs via quarterly cost forecasts. We established a protocol early on with our external actuaries and detailed our new culture, plans, strategies, and measures. Then, we kept actuaries fully in the loop with us by inviting them to our safety workshops, training sessions, and leadership meetings. We also met formally at least semiannually with the actuaries to update progress and hear any concerns they had. The CEO would always kick off those sessions to demonstrate commitment from the top.

5. **Hire an impartial set of eyes.** Use impartial outside audit firms to review your internal policies and procedures. No matter how strong your organizational commitment is to safety, you will run the risk of becoming blind to obvious shortcomings after spending enough time in your organization. It's human nature. A word of caution, however: your auditors will develop the same blind spots after the passage of time. If you hire the same auditors routinely to review compliance with your policies and procedures, they too can become comfortable. Accordingly, design the audit process to prevent friendships or personal relationships from forming between your auditor and employees. Use an audit firm with depth so that individual auditors are constantly rotated to review your organization.

CHAPTER 8:

Safety Is Leader Driven

The safety of the people shall be the highest law.
—Marcus Tullius Cicero

Is there a nobler professional calling than to lead others safely home? Is there any higher responsibility than to ensure we lead people home to their families? Greek philosopher Heraclitus is supposed to have said, "Out of every one hundred men on the battlefield, ten should not be there, eighty are nothing but targets, nine are fighters, and we are lucky to have them for they the battle make. Ah, but the one, one is a warrior, and he will bring the others home." Leadership requires a warrior ethos, and, as leaders, bringing people safely home is our duty.

As we stated in the introduction to this book and want to repeat here, *the leadership skills required to successfully manage safety are the same skills needed to manage top-notch operations: attention to detail, focused execution, standardized and disciplined processes, an understanding of roles, meaningful metrics, personal accountability, and alignment around the group mission and vision.* There is no "secret ingredient" that makes safety leadership different from overall organizational and operational leadership.

In an address at the 2007 Air Line Pilots Association International's Air Safety Forum, the Honorable Robert L. Sumwalt, NTSB Vice Chairman, said, "As aviation leaders, I suggest that you not only have the *ability* to influence safety, but you have the *obligation* to do so, as well. . . . Speaking up and saying something about . . . deviations is hard. It's unpopular. But, remember: 'All progress has resulted from people who took unpopular positions.' . . . If you accept anything less than standard, you send a message to others that it is okay to perform to a lower standard." As leaders, we have great capacity to directly impact lives. Not only do our decisions and actions involve our employees, but they also affect others close to those employees—spouses, children, parents, siblings, friends, and neighbors. It is, in the most basic terms, a privilege to lead people. However, it is also a formidable responsibility to create an energetic and positive culture of safety, especially in high-consequence scenarios.

There is no finish line to leadership. You're tested over and over again on your ability to lead others. In that, there are two main levers leaders have to effect change and drive performance: people and process. We have found fifteen management truths that serve as foundational elements in leading a culture of positive safety:

1. **This is not a grassroots affair.** A culture of positive safety must be leadership driven, but employee based. Waiting for a healthy safety culture to "bubble up" from the ranks is an ineffective strategy.

2. **This won't happen by chance.** Just like any other major program, instilling and sustaining a culture of positive safety requires a deliberate plan.

3. **A great safety culture is a journey.** It is not a destination. You will never achieve total safety. The benefit to the organization is achieved in the journey itself.

4. **Safety must be a core value of the enterprise.** Priorities change. Values don't change.

5. **Management must have courage to stay the course.** Disappointments will happen in the journey. Naysayers will be quick to claim defeat. Don't let it happen.

6. **Zero is the only acceptable goal.** Although 99.9 percent is a pretty good performance standard in most business arenas, it's not when it comes to safety.

7. **There must be organizational accountability for safety failures.** Blaming individuals at the front line without examination of organizational issues is the hallmark of unenlightened management.

8. **It is a low-cost solution.** No big-capital expenditures are needed. It is thinking and acting in a new way, where leaders set the example.

9. **Safety goes beyond compliance.** Regulations, rules, and laws are the baseline. Great safety requires individual commitment and personal accountability.

10. **Leaders should focus on execution, pay attention to detail, and not overcomplicate matters.** Execute the basics, and the battle is nearly won.

11. **The focus is on at-risk behaviors, not conditions.** Addressing behavior, not focusing exclusively on deficiencies in equipment or conditions, can prevent the majority of casualties.

12. **Safety is the ultimate organizational "North Star."** A foundational safety culture can help moderate typical internal and external distractions. It is the common ground on which people may freely rally to align with the mission.

13. **Safety success in the past doesn't guarantee safety success in the future.** There must be a leadership obsession with continuous improvement, or the organization risks stagnation.

14. **Safety requires solid SOPs.** Ensure SOPs are meaningful, clear, and followed.

15. **Rely on the principles of an SMS to frame the bones of your safety culture.** Having an SMS is a disciplined approach that we find beneficial for structuring a safety policy within four governance parameters: 1) *safe policy*—the doctrine, methods, processes, and organizational structure needed to meet safety goals; 2) *risk management*—the means to identify risks and how those risks will be managed; 3) *safety assurance*—the means to sustain performance and to identify and manage changing or new hazards; and 4) *safety promotion*—the means to integrate processes and policies into the safety culture.

We know that building a better business culture relies on engaging and empowering our employees. Their actions and behavior drive our culture. We set the course for a healthy culture, but our people bring it home. It's the same with building a culture of prevention.

No matter what we say or do to align our company with the understanding that safety is a core, nonnegotiable value, it doesn't matter unless our front lines are fully with us. If our employees fail to adopt safety as an ongoing commitment, it won't take long for the holes in the armor to show up. However, if our people get behind this mission, we are well on our way toward establishing the kind of safety culture that we want, and that will contribute to our bottom-line success.

All of this begins and ends with *your* leadership. Your team is concerned every time you have a situation, severe or not. You must perform a root cause analysis (discussed in chapter 20) on every issue, not just on those with costlier outcomes. You have to have a continuous unease in your organization to avoid complacent behaviors from setting in. In short, safety success depends on your ability to stand above the crowd and lead with conviction.

When we argue that safety is leader driven, we are not blurring the lines between leaders and managers. People often use the terms *leadership* and *management* interchangeably. This is a mistake. Being a manager is accompanied by a list of duties and responsibilities that can be defined and assigned. Being a leader is a trait that some people possess and that can be developed in others. Leadership has little to do with one's position in the organizational structure. Instead, leaders earn their respect and influence by their deeds.

A leader in your organization may be working with or against you. As you drive safety change in your organization, it is important to harness your leaders at all levels. These leaders have the influence to create desired behavior among the rest of your employees.

Fifteen Daily Safety Leadership Principles

1. **Lead.** Don't delegate safety. Be an example. You are on display every day.

2. **Execute.** Focus on execution of fundamentals.

3. **Manage.** Manage your high-risk situations and top three causes of casualties.

4. **Communicate.** Communicate your commitment and back it with actions.

5. **Seek input.** Encourage employee input. Take time to listen.

6. **Follow up.** Follow through on commitments and keep people posted.

7. **Be responsible.** Accept responsibility for the safety performance of your team.

8. **Make safety part of your daily plan.** Make safety an essential part of your business plan.

9. **Coach.** Mentor and lead employees in safety.

10. **Reinforce.** Positive reinforcement gets everyone involved.

11. **Promote advocacy.** Seek out and reward safety advocacy.

12. **Be consistent.** Safety is a daily focus—not just when convenient.

13. **Be impartial.** Administer discipline in an impartial, consistent, and predictable way.

14. **Seek root cause.** Support root cause investigation findings, even if painful.

15. **Put people first.** Be hard on facts, easy on people, to build a culture of trust.

CHAPTER 9:

Good Leadership Habits That Ensure Team Effectiveness

Stay the Course—Even When It Hurts

Consistency in values and message will define the sustainability of your culture. To your people, you are the owner of company culture. You are on display, and your people will do what they see you do, not necessarily what they hear you say. That is why it is important to stay the course and focus on taking care of issues that challenge the culture not only when everything is going right but particularly when the team is task saturated and prone to distraction. During such periods, it may seem more expedient to let problems go and hope for the best. But letting standards slip is dangerous, and the resulting cultural wavering tends to destroy morale. Being consistent, no matter the challenge at hand, goes a long way to anchor the right culture with employees and stakeholders.

There are many examples where we see leaders conceding their values and jeopardizing team loyalty. Perhaps one of the most visible examples in our society today occurs in athletics, particularly big-league college programs. The pressure to win may be so unyielding that deviant behaviors by key players may be overlooked despite conflicting with team values and team rules. For example, say that a star player violates team rules by missing a meeting or openly criticizing the coaches in public because he or she feels slighted by reduced playing time. Rather than standing firm on basic values, because he or she is a key player on the field, the coaching staff and administration look the other way. They fail to address the real issue: this one individual has put himself or herself above the good of the team. By letting standards slip they have sent a strong and clear message to everyone else that values are to be observed only when it benefits the circumstance. This guarantees loss of team essence and demotivation of the good people who follow the rules and put the team first.

There are a number of positive leadership habits that we have developed over decades in organizational life. None of these habits are new, but we believe all are worth consideration as part of the equation to keep a team healthy and focused.

1. **Never assume that things are fine.** Business life is dynamic and fluid. There will be change, and nothing stays the same. Heraclitus is believed to have said, "No man ever steps in the same river twice." Whether change is good or bad is up to you. You can't get complacent. Every day counts in nourishing solid team character. Good leaders constantly assess where their gaps are.

2. **Never take good employees for granted.** Never assume that they will always be there. Never compromise on baseline values, because team cohesion may be at stake if there is inconsistent messaging or action.

3. **Recognize that the organization will "talk" to you.** Listen and watch for signals that reveal the organizational climate. Reality is your friend. Pay attention and be quick to react if you sense that the culture is getting lazy.

4. **Have a plan.** Good processes and team alignment will not happen by winging it. Assess and reassess

the plan continuously and leave nothing to chance. Pay attention to details and insist on flawless execution of the basics.

5. **Personally engage.** Commit the time necessary to ensure that there is clarity around team roles and deliverables. Trust your people to do the job, and leverage collective team energy to fill possible organizational gaps.

6. **Realize that team alignment is never permanently fixed.** It is always under repair. Past success does not guarantee future success. Remember that the journey requires dedicated leadership energy.

7. **Understand the importance of instituting the right team architecture.** Regularly evaluate your people—their attitudes, capabilities, and suitability. You need the best people in the right places to maximize financial performance. Force ranking people is a healthy exercise. The process alone provides a number of positive results for a company. For one, ranking people ensures that you put the right people in the right seats. It also forces fence-sitters to get engaged or risk elimination, as well as helping you identify possible future management stars.

In summary, the lack of leadership engagement destroys any chance of instilling a culture of positive safety in a company. A lack of a healthy safety culture produces casualties to people and property, lost productivity, and financial underperformance. Perhaps just as significant is the potential collateral damage suffered through loss of social reputation and corporate credibility with customers, community, and other key stakeholder groups. Loss of reputation can be a going-out-of-business strategy. This was well pointed out in a 2015 Edelman study on corporate branding and reputation, involving research in ten countries with ten thousand respondents. The study revealed some sobering statistics about loss of brand value as a result primarily of safety failures and the companies' public responses to the failures.

CHAPTER 10:

Precision Execution: The Fighter Pilot Way

As a military fighter pilot, Jim learned early that he who executes with precision lives to fly another day. Military fighter pilots have certain methodologies that help them execute with accuracy. One of these methodologies is called "Precision Execution Process" (PEP). These principles can also help businesses achieve operational excellence. Like fighter aviation, companies that best execute in the competitive marketplace are those that prosper. We have used this approach successfully in transforming safety performance in organizations both large and small. We know that by instilling process discipline in your organization and following this or a similar template, you will drive elevated performance, eliminate departmental tendencies to silo, clarify group roles and deliverables, and better engage your team.

1. **Plan.** Convene the group and plan your strategy, tactics, roles, and metrics. Include your team in the planning to promote buy-in and individual ownership.

2. **Brief.** Communicate the plan to the team. Be specific with responsibilities, goals, and deliverables. Ensure people understand why yours is the right strategy.

3. **Execute.** Take the field and make it happen. With good execution of the first two steps (plan and brief), everyone should know what is expected, their role, and their deliverables.

4. **Debrief.** Reconvene the group and critique performance, outcomes, and benefits.

5. **Discuss lessons learned.** Pinpoint what worked and what didn't work.

6. **Apply to next mission.** Apply the lessons learned to the next project.

CHAPTER 11:

Create a Just Culture

There has been a lot written over the past few years about "just culture." There are many academics and others who have defined their perceptions of what a just culture means. For our purposes, we like the approach that considers just culture as a superior business model that differentiates companies through attributes that dramatically enable elevated organizational performance and potential financial advantage.

It is a balanced business standard that provides a variety of benefits:

- **Systemic accountability.** There should be accountability between designed management systems and the employees working inside those systems.

- **Workplace dignity and justice with a purpose.** It demonstrates in real time that the senior management is committed to living up to organizational values.

- **An employee-centric, values-supportive approach to customer service.** Most service initiatives place the customer as the principal focus. In this approach, excellent customer experience is a by-product of engaged employees working inside well-designed systems.

- **A coherent approach to operational performance improvement initiatives.** This optimizes return on investment through enterprise alignment and balancing competing business priorities in safety, human resources, risk, and logistics.

- **Improved labor relations and worker satisfaction.** Employees are respected as partners in achieving strategic alignment and stronger operational performance.

The Honorable Robert L. Sumwalt, NTSB, told us a story that made the point very well. Robert was leading a team investigating a major maritime accident. While he was reviewing what happened with management, the CEO told him, "Mr. Sumwalt, we have the problem totally fixed. We fired the captain in charge during the accident."

Robert considered that summary for a moment. Then he reminded management that this fired captain was a sixteen-year veteran with an impeccable record. Beyond that, he also had trained most of the other captains. Yes, the captain had made a mistake. Follow-up action was appropriate. But dismissing him from his job without considering the other individuals and policies that may have contributed to the accident didn't seem right. Yet, in management's view, there was blame to be assigned and punishment to be meted out. The captain would get the ax, and that was all there was to it.

We shook our heads as we reflected on this decision. It sure sounded to us like fairness and justice had been swept overboard. In fact, not only was this act unfair to the captain, it also sent an alarming message to everyone around him: if this captain could get fired as a reaction to an honest mistake, we're all on shaky ground around here!

This story is a compelling reminder that leaders and managers in a vibrant culture need to commit to infusing a sense of fairness and justice into their workplace environment, not only in executing major decisions, but in all their daily actions and interactions. Figuring out how to do that is really an art, not one ironclad rule written in a handbook.

There is another lesson here. The traditional way of improving safety—accident analysis—is not always the most suitable today in some industries. Accident and fatality rates in some groups, such as commercial aviation, nuclear power, some manufacturing, and others, has diminished to the point where meaningful forensic study of accident data is not the most effective way to continue active improvement. To be sure, when there is a failure in these industries, the consequences are usually severe. But, such events don't generally happen at a frequency that provides abundant data points to frame continuous safety progress.

So, how are we to take safety to the next level? Our experience is that voluntary employee disclosure of errors and mistakes is an increasingly important way to drive a culture of pure prevention. It is common sense that focusing on punishment for honest errors pushes real and often serious risk underground because people are afraid to disclose mistakes or "why" they did something. In contrast, the just culture way creates an atmosphere of trust where people are willing to report slipups or omissions without fear of reprisal. This, in turn, enables management to identify hidden trends and risks that lurk in the shadows waiting to happen. It provides an open pathway to greater safety because risks are identified and addressed before there is catastrophic failure. Management is able to focus resources where risks are greatest because they are known.

In a culture where fairness rules, decisions are made looking at all relevant factors as a whole: seniority, performance, attitude, behavior, and other considerations relevant to your company. Careful thought is given to each area. Of course, the severity of the action or offense needs to be held in a prominent place in these considerations. Swift action must be taken for gross violations of your core company values. Sometimes "one strike and you're out" is the fair and just guiding force in a decision. However, in many other situations, a different response is far more appropriate and effective. Coaching may take precedence over formal discipline in all but the most extreme cases of employee mistakes and offenses.

Practicing the tool of organizational accountability also can help shed light on contributing factors to what happened and identify any policies or procedures that need changing or updating to help ensure that similar problems and mistakes won't be repeated. The finger of blame is not frozen in the path of one individual.

The goal of leaders in a vibrant culture is for employees to know they will be treated fairly in any situation. By steering away from a rigid, rule-bound method of treating your employees and operating with a broader sense of fairness and justice, trust will grow. As trust grows, your bond with your employees also will blossom.

Over the last several years it has been encouraging to witness greater attention being given to what is often called a just culture in businesses and organizations. Certainly, any healthy business culture should also be a just culture where fairness and consistency steer the management of employees on every level. By investing your time in the creation of a just culture, *you are building an atmosphere of trust in which people are encouraged or even rewarded for speaking up about mistakes or problems, but in which they are also clear about where the line must be drawn between acceptable and unacceptable behaviors.*

Establishing a just culture takes more than following a relevant section of a handbook. It requires judgment, collaboration, and review. Sure, it's easier to whip out a form and treat every situation exactly the same. However, a cookie-cutter approach often creates a rigid, unjust environment. It also strips your managers of their judgment.

Let's look at an example. When Jim was VP and chief safety officer at CSX, there was disharmony between labor union leadership and railroad management. Discord had evolved over decades, and mistrust was rampant on both sides. The major issue from rail labor's view was what they considered an unjust discipline policy. There was no provision in the policy to distinguish between honest error and willful misconduct. In effect, everyone was subjected to the same punishment regardless of circumstances. Not until the discipline policy was fixed would there be a chance to heal the relationship. With both sides entrenched in their positions, the CEO asked Jim to find a fix. With that authority, Jim called in labor union leaders and select managers and facilitated a complete redo of the policy to make it more just. Coaching and peer intervention was the new course for unwillful and nonrepetitive situations. It was a hard process with a lot of give-and-take, but in the end the company benefitted with more trust and openness among the internal stakeholders through a nonreprisal approach (see a sample nonreprisal policy template later in this chapter).

This example underscores the need for building a sense of fairness through a broader, more effective approach. If you commit to being the guardian of a culture that supports a sense of fairness, keep these priorities in mind:

- Establish clear definitions about what is and is not acceptable behavior.

- Communicate your policies and standards clearly and consistently to your team.

- Empower management to follow consistent procedures for fully reviewing all mistakes, errors, and offenses where sanctions or penalties may be appropriate.

- Follow up on actions taken and decisions made with detailed reports shared with all appropriate parties.

Your own wisdom, experience, and creativity will further guide you toward outlining the fair and just foundation that will support your vibrant culture.

Now that we have established the basic principles of

a just culture, let's apply these concepts specifically to the creation of a healthy safety culture. These concepts were offered by K. Scott Griffith, founding partner and principal collaborator at SG Collaborative Solutions, LLC:

The Just Culture Methodology in Creating a Positive Culture of Safety

- A just culture model refers to a safety-supportive system of shared accountability where organizations are accountable for systems they have designed and responding to the behaviors of employees in a fair and just manner.

- In turn, employees are accountable for the quality of their choices and honest reporting of their actions, omissions, errors, and system vulnerabilities.

- This collective cultural standard is designed to help boost organizational performance by placing less focus on incidents, errors, and outcomes, and more focus on risk identification, system design, and the management of the behavioral choices of its people.

- In this model, errors and outcomes are the outputs to be monitored, while system design and behavioral choices are the inputs to be managed.

- Collaborative organizations recognize three major categories of human behavior and the importance of responding appropriately to each.

Category 1: Human error. Human error occurs when an individual inadvertently does other than what should have been done, that is, a slip, a lapse, or a mistake.

Organizations that practice just culture examine the human error rate of other individuals in these circumstances and seek to learn from reports, audits, and close calls before an accident occurs.

In a just culture, when a human error occurs, the response includes

- working with the person who made the mistake to assist in making better choices that will lower the likelihood of future errors, and

- evaluating the system or process to determine if a redesign will better identify and manage the risks involved.

Category 2: At-risk behavior. At-risk behavior involves making a choice that increases risk where risk is not recognized or is mistakenly believed to be justified.

In this culture, the response to at-risk behavior is similar to the response to human error, yet here exists the opportunity to more closely examine the choices themselves. When at-risk behavior occurs, the response includes

- coaching the person(s) about awareness of risk,

- removing barriers or disincentives to compliance with rules and procedures, and

- promoting incentives that produce desired behaviors.

Why not simply punish people who demonstrate at-risk behaviors? Actions such as rewarding outcome-based performance or looking the other way when no harm occurs may have inadvertently contributed to the presence of these at-risk behaviors. Punishing at-risk behavior serves to drive admission to or reporting of these choices below the surface, putting management at a disadvantage attempting to solve dysfunctional routines at the root of the behavior. Punishment in such circumstances results in hiding at-risk behavior.

Category 3: Reckless behavior. Reckless behavior is a choice to consciously disregard a substantial and unjustifiable risk.

The just culture response to reckless behavior is to quickly address the involved individual with punishment, discipline, or strong administrative action if there is conscious disregard of substantial rules and unjustifiable risk is taken. This has to be consistently applied, regardless of the actual outcome.

It's necessary to recognize the outcome bias and demonstrate a fierce intolerance for the reckless choice before actual harm occurs. (Category definition content courtesy of K. Scott Griffith, SG Collaborative Solutions.)

To demonstrate organizational commitment to just culture, some companies are adopting a nonreprisal policy that formalizes the strategy and clarifies organizational and individual responsibilities. The template that we have used coincides with a format similar to one provided to us by the Honorable Robert L. Sumwalt III.

Nonreprisal Policy

- **Our value.** Safety is the cornerstone value at [company name].

- **Our goal.** Our goal is zero injuries, accidents, and casualty events.

- **Our commitment.** We are committed to being the safest organization possible. Any task that cannot be done safely should not be attempted until it can be done safely.

- **Open reporting.** It is imperative that we have open, free, and good-faith reporting of any hazard, occurrence, or other information that in any way could impact the safety of operations.

- **Individual responsibility.** Every individual at [company name] is responsible for acting safely and reporting to any supervisor or manager information that may affect personal or process safety.

- **No reprisal.** To promote the timely, uninhibited flow of critical safety information, this process must be free of reprisal. Accordingly, [company name] will not use this reporting system to initiate administrative or disciplinary action against any individual who discloses in good faith information on a hazard or occurrence that results from conduct that is inadvertent, unintentional, or not deliberate, and that is not a pattern of behaviors or repeated misapplication of rules.

- **Expectation.** We expect that all [company name] personnel will endorse this program to help ensure our company continues to provide employees, customers, and communities the highest level of safety.

A JUST CULTURE

In a Just Culture, employees know that the company is committed to fairness. Just Culture is based on management judgment and not rigid rule driven handbooks.

CHAPTER 12:

Accidents Can Happen to the Best Companies: Are You Ready?

Building healthy safety culture is not for the weak. If you play in this arena long enough, odds are that you will see your share of disturbing accidents. We hope that the tools in this book will help you greatly mitigate this risk, but it would be foolish not to be prepared. You must deal with your own fears or anxiety, which could undermine your ability to lead your team in a bold new direction. The fear of a tragic accident or injury can be paralyzing. The tools in this book will allow you to rest a little bit easier, knowing that you have done everything in your control to prevent accidents. That said, it is important that you find ways to keep any fears at bay while focusing on sustaining the healthy culture you have begun to shape.

Sometimes our anxiety stems from mega-fears about the state of our companies, especially if something goes wrong. Sometimes fears emerge from our personal lives. These fears frequently crop up because we are not adequately protected against calamities.

When you are worried about all the things that could go wrong, you can't lead your business with a clear head. That means you can't grow and protect your culture, either. You risk being too distracted to implement and continue to use these culture-building tools. Something else threatens to cast a larger shadow over your day-to-day leadership.

Therefore, it's vital to find ways to head off these crippling fears. The old saying that "the best offense is a good defense" is true and relevant here. Take the precautionary measures that can stop these fears before they show up.

Based on our own experience and what we have seen with countless other leaders and companies of all sizes, here are some typical realms where it pays to execute defensive maneuvers:

- **Make sure you have adequate personal insurance.** You need to feel confident that you will be covered if you are sued personally as the result of your acts or omissions in the performance of your corporate duties. Carry a personal umbrella with limits, depending on your individual factors. In today's world, $10 million should be the least you consider. If your business is set up right, you should not be personally liable. Still, that won't prevent someone from suing you personally, and it may not prevent a jury from piercing through the company if its assets are not sufficient to handle the claim. Don't get caught relying on theory rather than reality. Protect yourself against reality.

- **Take out solid directors and officers (D&O) liability insurance, as well as employer's liability insurance.** You're not the only individual in your company who could be named in a suit, and you need to be prepared. When choosing your coverage, don't simply land on a nice round number. Carry the limits that most closely match your worst-case assessment.

- **Take active steps to keep your personal assets and business assets out of reach of creditors if your business should fail.** Talk to an experienced estate planning attorney to strategize the best options to put certain personal assets in trust so creditors can't get at them. This is not something you should entrust your general attorney to handle. Find an estate planner with experience working with business people, someone who does not need to be educated about the risks or the action steps to avoid them.

- **Similarly, if you have multiple businesses inside one company with different risk profiles, divide the businesses into separate companies.** If you have an asset-heavy company with operating risk, consider forming a leasing company to lease the assets to the operating company. Complicated? Maybe. Fee intensive? Often. However, if everything blows up, you will feel pretty good that you have protected your company and your shareholders.

- **Insure for the worst-case scenario to the extent allowed by your budget.** Don't view insurance as existing to take care of the small paper cuts. Insurance is there for a potentially severe accident. Having $2 million in general liability insurance sounds like extensive coverage. In reality, it is a drop in the bucket under the wrong scenario. Buy as much umbrella coverage as needed to protect against a reasonable worst case. Consider taking more front-end risk (e.g., greater deductibles) in exchange for higher coverage limits. Large insurance limits will allow you to think more clearly, knowing that a major accident or injury is less likely to threaten your business's existence.

- **Most importantly, have a disaster plan prepared in detail.** If tragedy strikes, you need to begin execution mode immediately and 24/7. This is not the time to be asking, "What should we do now?"

You and your entire leadership team must know in detail who is responsible for each aspect of managing the crisis. Ensure that your team includes the right people inside your company as well as properly qualified attorneys, adjusters, and public relations managers. At the same time, understand that the incident is likely to be a distraction for your team, your customers, and possibly the public. Make certain that your disaster plan includes a commitment to transparently communicate the issue to your employees and to allow those not involved in its resolution to return to work with clear minds. The incident, no matter how severe, cannot derail the rest of your business.

Feel free to add to this list any other subjects or areas where you recognize the need to play defense to keep your fears from blocking your way in successfully leading your company and your culture. What are the worst-case scenarios that dance across your mind or keep you up at night?

Taking the time now to play some defense may be just what you need to keep focusing on your mission to build a better safety culture and achieve greater profitability and success for your company. You need to be asking yourself every day, "What else can I do to sustain and enhance our company's safety culture right now?" To successfully accomplish this, you must have a clear head, knowing that your downside is protected.

CHAPTER 13:

Safety Is Employee Owned

A vibrant culture is the result of effectively managing attitude, philosophy, and behavior. When it comes to leading the way on safety in your organization, you need to maintain a constant emphasis on managing the *behavior* of your people. Even when you engage and empower your people in the overall process of naming and enforcing safety procedures and operations, human behavior will always enter into the equation. At every step of the way, it is up to you and your key managers to help manage that behavior. In a culture of prevention, behavior trumps rules and regulations.

This begins with our own culture perceptions. When we think of compliance in the United States, we often think of following the rules and regulations. A while ago, as Brian was in New Zealand preparing to present one of his workshops on building a vibrant culture, he came across an eye-opening reference from the Māori, the indigenous Polynesian people of that country. The Māori have a term for compliance—*tikanga*—which means "the way we do things; who we are." It's a spiritual approach that requires the buy-in of all participants. It's about values, and it's about *behavior*. Maybe we need to think more like the Māori. Our commitment to *tikanga* defines who we are organically, not via rule making.

In 2014, a truck plowed into the limo of actor Tracy Morgan, killing a passenger and severely injuring Morgan. As it turned out, NTSB findings documented that the truck driver was in compliance with regulations regarding appropriate working hours: he had not exceeded legal driving hours. However, the press reported that the truck driver had pulled an all-nighter on his own time the night before getting into his truck. If true, no regulation could have prevented that driver from getting behind the wheel when he was already exhausted. As documented by investigators and reported widely, poor decisions and behaviors played a role in the cause of this accident.

Promoting safety is tantamount to promoting individual accountability. In other words, *the key for any employee in upholding a culture of prevention is making the right choices, even when no one is looking!*

As leaders, we need to consistently enforce this message. We must demonstrate, teach, and manage acceptable safety behaviors, not just compliance with rules and regulations. An individual accident or injury, no matter how serious, does not simply happen. It is most likely the result of a series of unsafe behaviors that have gone undetected and without remedy. Perhaps an employee was properly trained but failed to follow safety procedures. Maybe the employee improvised in contravention of safety policy, cutting corners to save time or money and thereby causing something to backfire.

That employee should face appropriate consequences and be provided coaching and training to realign with your safety mission. However, it's all too easy to simply blame a frontline employee or supervisor for a safety-related accident. We need to look further. As we hold our employees individually accountable for safety results, we also must create team and organizational accountability. We must be our own harshest critics, unafraid to examine our own processes and procedures continually, organization-wide, with the goal of continuous improvement in regard to safety. Ask the tough questions:

- Did the accident result from a lack of communication or inadequate training about operating procedures or safety steps?

- Did faulty or nonexistent auditing of systems contribute to the incident?

- Was there a lack of institutional memory, meaning that an earlier mistake or incident by one or more employees was not thoroughly addressed and was therefore repeated through another employee's actions?

Leaders must commit to doing everything in their power to ensure that similar mistakes never happen again. In a culture of prevention where behavior is effectively managed, a fatigued equipment operator, driver, pilot, captain, or any employee with responsibility over an operation is empowered to stop for any safety-related reason without fear of retribution.

You should be prepared to make the same kind of thorough evaluation, review, and redirection after *any* kind of accident or safety mishap. Yes, accidents can happen. None of us are immune. In a culture of prevention, though, our primary goal is to *prevent* accidents before they happen. That means effectively managing the behavior of your employees, even before trouble arises.

Look at this accident pyramid. On average, thirty thousand unsafe decisions and conditions result in three thousand minor accidents, three hundred accidents that result in some sort of lost time with medical treatment, thirty disablements, and one fatality. Where do you want to spend your time? Do you want to spend it on the fatality and disablements? We don't think so. You want to spend your time at the base of the pyramid focusing on the unsafe conditions and decisions that lead up to the disablements and the fatality.

What is at the base of the pyramid? Behavior. To create a culture of prevention, we must focus on decision-making and behavior so that people are empowered to make the right decisions and to err on the side of safety. If you spend your time worried about fatalities and disablements, you are chasing the animals that have escaped the farm, and all you're going to do is spend your time on more and more animals that escape. If you really want to spend your time eliminating or reducing accidents as much as possible, focus on behavior.

CHAPTER 14:

Hire and Integrate the Right People for Your Safety Culture

If a vibrant company culture is the right people and the right processes working in harmony with employee ownership at the foundation, then it's critical that you devote extra care and attention to hiring with your culture in mind. If you hire people who don't fit your culture and won't support it, you will be undermining your mission.

Does that mean that skills and abilities are no longer important when interviewing and selecting job candidates? Of course not. Hiring the right people certainly requires finding those who are technically well qualified. At the same time, recognize that the hiring process is a valuable opportunity for you to act within alignment with your company culture and take proactive steps to enhance it over time.

When evaluating potential new employees, keep these questions in mind:

- Do they share your company values?

- Do they seem to understand the flavor and tone of your company culture and resonate with it?

- What kinds of company cultures, good or bad, have they worked in previously, and how does that influence what they seek in a new company culture?

- How well do they seem to understand and value teamwork, both as it relates to the execution of job tasks and the needs of your culture?

- During the interview process, to what extent do they demonstrate the kinds of characteristics that will support your culture?

Questions like these will add an extra dimension to your own basic hiring procedures.

During the interview process, be sure to go beyond the candidates' skills and employment history. Include screening questions designed to assess your candidates' behavior in the workplace: How do they handle stress? How do they deal with strained or difficult communications with others?

The more eyes looking closely at a job candidate, the more likely it is that someone will pick up on something that just doesn't click. One person in a group can prevent the company from making a bad hire.

Move beyond orientation to integration. In a vibrant culture, your current employees will pick up where the formal orientation left off and guide your new employees through the informal integration. In an unhealthy culture, informal integration takes the form of telling new employees how to stay out of trouble, when to keep their mouth shut, whom they should avoid—we all know that drill. In a healthy culture, the picture of the informal integration looks different. Your new employees learn that values such as respect, teamwork, and integrity really matter at your company. Your opinion leaders fulfill their role of driving the culture home and setting the right tone with their positive attitude and affirming comments. In one way or another, your team is conveying a spirit that says, "We like working here, and we trust that you will too."

Develop a mentoring program. Mentoring is another way that your team can assist new hires in the integration process. Informal mentoring can be helpful, but a more structured mentoring program may be especially effective in steering your new employees toward successful job performance and a smooth integration into your team. Find the best approach for your company: one-on-one mentoring or a mentoring circle with a group of employees. Consider where senior management should be involved or where peer-to-peer mentoring would be more productive. Choose your mentor-mentee matches carefully, and conduct an orientation program for participants on effective mentoring.

While we want new employees to help sustain our vibrant culture, we also need to recognize that our culture is constantly evolving. The truth is that each hire will bring something new to the table. You support that reality by demonstrating to new team members the open channels of communication and receptiveness to creative ideas that are part of the foundation of your culture.

CHAPTER 15:

Rethink the Role of Your Managers

A safety culture must be driven by the company's top leadership. It must be owned by the whole organization, including the front lines. But what about your managers? They are a critically important piece of the puzzle. After all, they are charged with the execution of the components of your safety culture. Managers get a bad rap. Too often, they're blamed when things go wrong in the workplace. In reality, the manager is among our most valuable resources. The manager is the conduit to ensuring our safety goals and behaviors penetrate the entire company.

Unfortunately and unfairly, the manager takes the blame for the shortcomings of how many companies are structured. While we must attack wasteful structures, processes, and positions, the role of the manager must be re-tooled for today's organization. Let's put our managers in the position to ignite our safety culture by understanding the following concepts:

- **Managers are not the problem.** Our own inefficiencies and bureaucracies are the problem. If we put the manager in an organization that is designed (intentionally or not) to maintain the status quo, kill creativity, and fear decision-making, why are we surprised when the manager exhibits this behavior too? The "micro-manager" is often a symptom of an organization that is perfectly designed to generate this result by not promoting a culture of empowerment and by not giving the manager the tools and training to develop his or her team. Blaming the manager ignores the real issue, which is that many businesses operate using antiquated "command and control" philosophies.

- **Many businesses fail to articulate organizational clarity, regardless of structure.** Managers often are vested with responsibility but lack proper authority or tools to execute on the company's strategic objectives. At this point, managers justifiably are frustrated, and that frustration spills to the front lines. Once again, the problem is not with the manager per se; it's with the company's failure to communicate structures, values, and accountability and appropriately empower its managers.

- **Some companies offer little to no training in how to develop managers, how to clearly communicate, how to promote accountability, and how to lead.** And again, is this the manager's problem, or is it a problem in how executives develop them? Consider that many managers were promoted from front-line positions due to their work ethics and technical competencies. These attributes don't necessarily prepare someone to manage people in today's business environment. The hiring of managers via promotion from within will work best if there is an accompanying plan to develop the high-potential employee into an effective leader of people first and foremost. Somehow, many of us have bought into the contrast between a "leader" and "manager." In reality, our best managers are leaders. Are we making the appropriate effort to groom our managers into leaders?

- **Today's manager is the key to ensuring that your safety culture permeates throughout the entire business.** A healthy safety culture is about the right behaviors, philosophies, and attitudes. Our cultures must be leader driven and employee owned. Today's manager ensures that all employees are aligned with the company's values, strategy, and mission. Today's manager looks beyond technical skills and key performance indicators to ensure that unwanted behaviors are eliminated from the company (i.e., lack of empowerment, status-quo thinking, and micromanaging). Today's manager establishes trust as the foundation of all relationships.

Appropriately trained and aligned managers are vital to the execution of the company's mission and to the development of employees. Having the right people in management roles will accelerate the development and anchoring of your safety culture.

CHAPTER 16:

Take Your Front Lines with You

Sometimes it's difficult for us as business leaders to admit that we don't have all the answers. Yet the reality is that we face many situations and decisions where we need to turn to other people and resources for ideas, guidance, or suggestions. Pretending that we always know what's right only gets us into trouble.

This is definitely true when it comes to changing our business culture. Nothing turns off employees faster than sensing that their leader has assumed he or she knows exactly what's wrong and, without seeking their input, is charging full speed into his or her own secretly hatched plan. Do not make this mistake. Take a different approach. Make it a regular practice to gather feedback and ideas from your team.

One effective way to do that is to bring your employees together and engage them in an exercise called "CEO for a Day." You can call upon this exercise at any time to address any specific problem or issue that appears to be sabotaging your company's performance or workplace environment. Jetco used this resource to ask its team what we were going to do to improve employee retention and further drive safe behaviors. The results were even better than we imagined, generating tangible ideas that turned the tide on the problem and enhanced employee ownership of the process. You can definitely use this tool as an effective means of setting your course on your safety culture.

Let's go through the exercise step by step:

Step 1: Talk to your employees. Admit that just because you are the CEO or president, you really don't have all the solutions. You may not even have *most* of the solutions. You believe that your team has the best answers, and you're eager to hear them. Your front lines are your most valuable, but most often overlooked, asset. They have many great ideas if you take the time to listen to them.

To help them get started, frame one question to focus on. Avoid questions that can be answered with a *yes* or *no*. You don't have to make it as direct as "How do we change our culture?" That's one option, but it may sound too broad or all-encompassing to your employees (unless they've read this book!). They might respond more readily to questions related to key aspects of your culture:

- How do we improve morale?
- How do we make our company a great place to work?
- How can we build a stronger, more cohesive team?
- What are the values that we commit to live by?

You will most likely know the most effective way to get the conversation going, and if your first attempt at naming the question to answer does not engage your team, listen for clues from them to revise it to land on a subject they have a whole lot to say about.

Step 2: Solicit your team's direct feedback on the agreed-upon question. We suggest doing this through an anonymous survey format, one that allows your employees a few minutes to put their thoughts into writing rather than feeling forced to stand up and speak in front of you and all their peers without time to prepare. You are more likely to receive honest, open responses.

As you collect these replies, try not to correct them except for small changes to improve clarity or smooth out rough grammar. Even if you notice a totally impractical idea or suggestion, keep it in there. The person who wrote that response will see how his or her peers receive it in Step 3.

Step 3: Bring your team back together to share and discuss all their responses. Small breakout groups will usually facilitate a more productive discussion. Direct each group to evaluate all the responses and to select the ones that will best help your company address the problem or issue named in the opening question. Don't worry if strong feelings bubble up. Trust that your employees are finding their way to truthful, substantive responses that will lead to positive changes in your company.

Move the discussion toward a vote. When we lead this exercise, we list all the responses from the survey on flip-chart-sized pages attached to the wall. Give participants four black sticky dots and one red sticky dot. Tell them to attach the red dot to the single best idea with the black dots going to the next four most effective ideas. With a scoring system of one point for each black dot and three points for each red dot, you total the points. You can expect the votes to cluster around a tight handful of ideas.

Next, identify the top five ideas as voted upon by your team. Lead a discussion about how your team will implement these ideas, who is responsible, and the time frame for completion. Remind your employees that an idea is useless without a firm execution plan. Then, assign small working groups to implement each idea.

Step 4: Implement the prioritized ideas. After mostly stepping back during the survey and sorting out the responses, you will likely need to assume more of a facilitating role here. Teach people how to operationalize the ideas that they believe will improve morale or do whatever it is they set out to accomplish. Use your experience as leader to provide guidance on how to turn a goal into a reality, but empower your team to fully execute their plan. This is an important step in empowering your employees to be a part of changing your company culture.

When the Jetco team followed this exercise to address how to improve retention, the top idea that emerged was to form a driver committee and make sure it had a place in every important company meeting. The Jetco Driver Committee (DC) was founded to serve as the voice of our men and women on the road. Peers elect committee members, and a representative from the DC is present at every operations meeting. This change increased the sense of ownership among drivers, the heartbeat of the company; it also helped knock down the silos that kept divisions and groups apart. Tearing down silos is an essential part of building a business safety culture.

Step 5: Celebrate your success. Give your participants credit for inspiring a change that is improving your workplace environment.

There's an added bonus from conducting this exercise. As well as developing tangible ideas that will aid in your culture intervention, the CEO for a Day experience itself can serve as a catalyst for your team's more consistent engagement. "You had the ideas of how to deal with our problems all along," you remind them. Now, encourage them to create and sustain that sense of empowerment not just for one day, but every day. The exercise introduced them to this concept: you are empowered, you know what to do, and you have the tools.

TAKE YOUR FRONT LINES WITH YOU!

Be sure your meetings allow time for listening. Lectures simply do not work. People need to be heard before they can hear. This is especially true for your frontline employees who are often not heard.

CHAPTER 17:

Get into Their Hearts Before You Get into Their Heads

Building an empowered workforce is critical to the success of any business, and it's a vital part of creating and sustaining a vibrant culture. You want your employees to take ownership of their jobs, their roles, and their responsibilities. You want them to feel that they can appropriately make hands-on decisions and use their discretion in handling problems or issues that arise rather than relying on managers to shadow them on every step they take.

However, it's important to first understand this concept: *To have an empowered team, you first need to have an* engaged *team. The most effective way to engage your employees is to get into their hearts before you get into their heads.*

People have to be heard before they can hear. Your employees need to have a clear and solid sense that they are a vital part of who you are as a company, that they are relevant to what you're doing and how and why you're doing it. They need to feel that they belong, that they are included in your mission and your culture, and that what they are doing is making a difference. Unfortunately, many business leaders operate in a way that promotes a sense of exclusion, which gets in the way of building a fully engaged team. Here are two examples:

1. A company holds a meeting to strategize how to approach a problem but invites only the top team or perhaps one or two levels below. That means leaving out the front lines: production workers,

customer service representatives, warehouse staff, etc. If these frontline employees are nowhere to be found in planning meetings, how can they feel included and engaged in the company's operations and the reasons behind them?

2. Management runs off on a private retreat. The rest of the team is left behind. The message? You don't belong, and you are not important.

Leaders and managers who exclude their front lines in this way are being driven by the mistaken notion that they are smarter than their employees and that their job is to "enlighten" them. That kind of centuries-old thinking is obsolete. It has no place in a healthy culture and a successful business. Not only does such arrogance and exclusion undermine the sense of engagement that our employees need, it also limits our potential for finding creative and effective solutions to problems. Our employees on the front lines often know better than anyone else what's causing the problems our company is facing. If they are involved from the outset, they can lead the way toward a solution while feeling good about themselves and their company.

Leaders who successfully build a healthy culture understand that a well-functioning organization with a vibrant culture is much less a hierarchy than a holistic team of integrated groups working together for the common good. That not only makes business sense, it also makes "people" sense. If there is one lesson we have learned, it is that regardless of our title, position, education, personal background, status, or income, we all have the same basic needs: to be included, respected, and appreciated.

You can try to tell your employees, "We are all a team here," but that's an attempt to get into their heads before you get into their hearts. The more effective approach is to show your people that you respect them, that you appreciate them, that you're committed to being transparent with respect to everything that affects them. That's how you get into their hearts before you get into their heads. You are helping to meet those basic human needs. You are also creating a stronger internal base of support because your employees really do feel engaged. They know they matter, that they are important.

Leaders and managers also demonstrate that their employees really matter when they show authentic care for them. As we emphasized in an earlier tool, *employees notice and appreciate when we treat them as human beings first and employees second.*

A while ago, the Jetco team shared a group email. It was a personal shout-out for a manager of our drivers. As the driver who sent the email tells the story, he had spoken with his manager about his father a couple of weeks earlier. The next time the manager saw this driver he immediately asked him about his father. "I didn't really expect that he would remember, but he did," the driver explained. "I just want everybody to know how much that meant to me and my family."

You can bet this driver walked away from that experience feeling more engaged in his work and his place in the company. When Brian read the email, he was reminded that the supervisor-employee relationship is sacred. We believe that, to a large extent, employees stay with their managers, not their companies, and that they leave their managers, not their companies. By getting into his drivers' hearts through his caring and respect, this manager was winning the kind of loyalty that improves employee retention and strengthens company culture. A manager can tell his employees, "Your welfare really matters to me," but that's just an attempt to get into their heads. The message does not come through unless it's backed by sincere behavior.

Here's another example. You are seeking the most effective manner to convey the need for a particular change. You can lead with logic, calling upon facts and concrete strategies or ideas to articulate your case in a tightly structured presentation, but will that engage your team? Not necessarily. Sure, you need to be logical and reasoned in explaining the issue and what your company needs to do about it. However, responding to logic is not the way most human beings are wired. They need to be reached on a more personal level first.

When Brian called the team at Jetco together to address the growing number of accidents several years ago, he didn't start with the statistics. He began with an image: an explicit and frightening photo of an auto–truck accident (not at Jetco) where precious lives were lost. "Wow, we could have killed somebody!" our employees communicated through words and facial expressions. From then on the discussion of our need to deepen our commitment to safety unfolded on more productive ground. Our whole team had been fully engaged in the mission because that photo had shot right into their hearts.

CHAPTER 18:

Drive Your Culture Home—Literally

As Jetco has anchored its safety culture, we have learned that getting through to our employees is simply the beginning of the mission. If you focus on your employees and ignore their families, full cultural alignment is nearly impossible. The whole family must be engaged in the company's safety mission.

Here's why: in today's world, our family and friends are never more than a text, tweet, or Facebook message away. You want your employee's head to be fully in the game as he or she performs his or her mission's critical duties for your organization. This may be challenging if a demanding family member or friend is continually in contact.

What are your choices? Restrict Internet access? With smartphones, the employee probably does not need your Internet anyway. Check in all mobile devices at the beginning of the work day? Not happening.

The only way to ensure that your employees are able to put their full time and focus into safe execution is to ensure that their families are fully in line with your culture. How do you bring the families into the culture? Skip the hated annual company picnic. At their best, picnics might involve a hot dog, a carnival ride, and a fast exit. At their worst, everyone must attend but nobody *wants* to attend.

Instead, try these ideas:

- **Make regular contact instead of the annual show.** As an example, Jetco sends a monthly mailing to employees' homes. The mailing focuses on topics that are of general interest but that also have a clear tie into the company's values and mission. At Jetco, we might discuss using a hand-held phone while driving a truck is both dangerous and a violation of federal law. In the home mailing, we focus on the dangers of our employees and their children texting and driving.

- **Stage company events at your location.** How many times do our families really get to see how their loved ones spend the majority of their waking hours? Allow for "show-and-tell." This will tie everyone into a positive experience at your facility and help the family members understand the organization's direction. If you propose this idea and encounter significant resistance, it might be a strong suggestion that you need to look into the level of employee pride and alignment.

- **Be liberal when sharing information about the strengths and challenges of your company.** Help people understand that they are on a winning team. Be sure the whole family is engaged in the company's mission and understands the challenges faced by the company.

- **Be sure you are providing an outstanding company work environment.** Can a supportive family member help the employee compare what you offer to the "devil that you do not know"? Be sure the whole family knows what you offer in terms of intangibles, such as a happy, desirable place to work.

From an emotional, financial, and business perspective, anchoring your safety culture must involve frequent, repetitive, and focused contact not only with the people you see every day, but also with employees' family members. Executed correctly, you will have a whole army working to build and support your company's safety culture. For example, take a look at the letter below that was sent to the Jetco families. It asked the children related to Jetco family members to draw what "Driving to Perfection"—Jetco's internal culture that puts safety above all else—means to them. This exercise was an easy way to see that the culture had made it all the way to the families, based on the artwork received. Eventually, this became Jetco's calendar, which was distributed to not only Jetco customers, but to employees too.

ENGAGE THE FAMILY

Get into your employees' homes. Culture is about engaging the whole family. We are never more than a text message away from our loved ones, and family members must be aligned with our mission.

ENGAGE
THE FAMILY

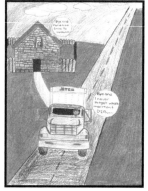

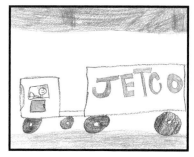

*We asked our employees' young relatives
to draw what Driving to Perfection meant to them.
We received outstanding replies and created a
company calendar—further engraining our culture at
home, at work, and with our customers.*

CHAPTER 19:

Never Dismiss a Minor Accident

In an unhealthy culture, employees cut corners because the company's values and processes are not understood or are out of alignment. As a leader, you must first communicate clearly that safety is a nonnegotiable value. Then you need to take the message further. Make it clear to them that if any employee sees a safety problem, a near miss, or concern anywhere in your company's operations, he or she should immediately throw the red flag until the team addresses the issue. Your people should always know the right action to take without fear of retribution. Even if the employee was wrong in his or her assessment, thank that person for calling a critical time-out. If disciplined, the employee will learn to never do so again.

All of us have been pushed to meet a deadline or to operate within a budget, but what should we do if meeting that deadline or budget would force us to violate the law or put people at risk? In a culture of prevention, nobody on your team has to think about that answer. Making the right choice becomes part of their DNA.

- **Help your employees adopt the mindset that when it comes to safety, zero is the only goal.** If you and your team accept one accident, you might as well accept a thousand. This is a common mistake companies make when tracking and assessing their safety record. They assume that if safety incidents drop by a certain percentage, everything is going well. They rationalize one or more issues by repeating the explanation, "Accidents happen." You and your employees need to live by a different attitude: *safety is an internal commitment carried by every individual, at all times.*

- **Promote an understanding that there is no such thing as a "minor" accident.** Shrugging off even one accident because it didn't have cataclysmic results is a surefire way to sabotage your culture of prevention. Just because no major damage to people or property resulted from a particular accident or safety incident does not mean it is not worthy of your time and reflection. Consider this example: "Hey, boss, I backed into a pole. There was no damage. What's the big deal?" Our reply: "To us, that pole looks to be about the same height as a five-year-old child. You just got lucky you hit a pole and not a child. It's that simple." The failure is in behavior. The driver didn't get out and look or check the circumstances before moving the vehicle. That he hit a pole and not a child means it was his lucky day, and had he hit a child, the discussion would be vastly different. This is a trucking example, but you can take this example and translate it to any one of your businesses.

As a leader you need to embody the attitude that there really is no such event as a minor accident. Severity is a matter of luck—nothing more, nothing less. Make it clear that in your company or organization, every incident merits full attention and swift follow-up. That commitment begins with you, and every employee on your team needs to embrace and follow it.

NEVER DISMISS AN ACCIDENT OR INJURY BECAUSE IT WAS MINOR

If an accident or injury was minor, it was your lucky day. Treat each incident as if it were severe. If you discount minor incidents, you are just buying time until the "big one" happens.

CHAPTER 20:

A Root Cause Analysis Is Essential— Regardless of Severity

A root cause analysis (RCA) is the best way to determine how to prevent future accidents. An RCA does not need to be a complex process. It simply allows you to get to the bottom of what happened.

Performing an RCA regardless of the severity produces two benefits. First, it will enable you to determine the cause *before* another accident happens. Second, it will create an intellectual rigor among your employees that can benefit all areas of your organization.

An RCA will help you understand how to continuously improve. You can't fix a problem if you don't understand its cause. When you understand why a failure occurred, then you can begin to make the needed systemic corrections. Without understanding the why, you are simply taking a wild guess as to the underlying cause—or putting a Band-Aid on the apparent problem.

In the spirit of keeping it simple, you can use these six steps to perform an RCA on virtually any incident worthy of investigation:

1. **Describe the incident.** What happened? How often has it happened?

2. **Investigate the incident.** Assign cross-functional teams to investigate. Ensure each team produces documentation to support its findings. This may require meetings with people both inside and outside the company.

3. **Investigate the process.** What process was supposed to be followed? Was it followed? If not, define where processes were not followed and why. Look especially for organizational versus individual failures.

4. **Define solutions based on the investigation.** Ensure the solutions are both practical and highly tailored to the incident.

5. **Formulate a plan.** Once the solution is defined, what is the action plan for implementation and measurement of success? Who, what, where, when, and how? Communicate the final plan to your whole team; institutionalize the knowledge.

6. **Document and test.** Document the resolution and test periodically to ensure that the resolution was correct and has taken hold.

The RCA is your best means to ensure lasting prevention. Pointing fingers and casting blame only buys time until the same problem arises again.

CHAPTER 21:

Create an Internal Brand around Safety

As entrepreneurs, we spend a fortune working on our brand. We wonder whether our customers understand our value proposition or if it is too narrow or broad. Does our logo represent who we are? How about our ads—are they getting the message across? We hire marketing firms and consultants to demonstrate how we are different from our competition and why it matters, but most of our marketing effort is *outwardly* focused.

As important as it is to have a well-known external brand to draw customers, it's equally important to ensure your brand values exist *inside* your organization. Your internal brand is your rallying cry. Every employee must know what the brand represents and be able to break it down through a concise summary of your company's culture and values.

Jetco's internal brand is "Driving to Perfection" (D2P). That is the Jetco way. The company has a logo and video testimonials to support the brand, and it appears on all employee correspondence and promotional items. Jetco has discussed it enough among our employees that if visitors ask anyone in our company what D2P means, they will get consistent answers.

Some of the testimony in company produced videos in support of D2P is especially heartwarming. It shows employees discussing how previous employers pressured them to cut corners. They go on to explain that, within Jetco's culture, they have the freedom to do their work the right way. Employees even discuss how they have taken our company values into their personal lives. For example, one individual told how he used D2P when teaching his kids to drive.

An internal brand is a convenient vehicle with which to concisely repeat value-based messages several times per day.

Once you have built your internal brand and it is well understood, you can have some fun. Creative awards, T-shirts, and recognition programs all are effective ways to build momentum for your new culture. The list of possibilities is endless for how you can promote your internal brand of culture and values to your team. However, remember: when developing an internal brand, the executives might lead the effort, but employees clearly drive the brand itself on a daily basis. Your employees are your brand ambassadors.

To create buy-in throughout the organization, Jetco created a contest. Management laid out the challenge: to develop a visual rallying cry that summarizes the company's culture and values. Leadership received dozens of great ideas. From there, teams narrowed the list down to five ideas that were presented to the entire company and then voted upon. Management led the process, but the employees owned and developed it.

Now, D2P permeates Jetco. It is the first thing drivers see when entering their truck cabs and the last thing they see when exiting. D2P is a constant reminder of who Jetco is as a company and what values we represent. However, while the constant visual reminders are important, success comes only by pairing words and images with consistent action throughout the organization. Our success using D2P as a rallying point for our entire organization is undeniable, but there certainly are many other effective internal branding campaigns.

While we were working for Waste Management Inc. (WM), Jim led a team that developed a comprehensive safety program called "Mission to Zero" (M2Z©). M2Z was the overarching strategy to transform the safety culture. There was a clear awakening that safety needed a renewed commitment throughout the company. The new CEO, Maury Myers, made it a principal focus. He recognized the human and financial toll poor safety had on WM people, customers, communities, and shareholders. He said, "Safety isn't just good business, it is the right thing to do." Jim and his team didn't spend their time simply creating handbooks and manuals that no one would read. Instead, they focused on culture and the need to drive values all the way to the front line. M2Z was the product of a comprehensive series of related programs, strategies, tactics, measures, and hands-on training and certification initiatives intended to promote value-based, safe behavior.

One of the cornerstones of M2Z was a program called "Life Changer" that included a video that told the story of a tragedy caused by the reckless conduct of a WM truck driver and a management team that was wholly disengaged and unsupportive. The culmination of horrible decisions all around led to the needless and tragic fatality of a remarkable young family man, Erich, who had been on a career fast track. His calling was to help people through improved health and physical fitness. The license plate on his car read "LIFCHGR." He wanted to be a life changer.

WM did not deny the errors and mismanagement of the local team or quietly sweep the accident under the rug like many companies would have done. WM stepped up, admitted fault, and pledged not to let the event go unremembered, actually partnering with Erich's widow, Heidi. Heidi, a magnificent spirit of forgiveness and integrity, helped to document the awful details and tell the story to every WM employee in hopes that it might prevent a similar occurrence elsewhere.

WM also created an annual Life Changer award in memory and honor of Erich. Heidi remained actively involved in the company program and presented the Life Changer awards at the company's annual leadership conferences. When she spoke about the tragedy to the WM team assembled, there was not a dry eye in the room. It was humbling to watch a typically alpha-personality group of people accept responsibility for the tragedy and vow to never let it happen again.

Using Life Changer to influence the company culture was a resounding success for WM because it recognized this important truth: beliefs and emotions trump logic. It would have been far easier and less risky had the company remained behind closed doors in isolation and studied statistics or created policies and handbooks, with little or no impact. Instead, Life Changer was based on personal emotion—the recognition that our organization had needlessly caused a tragedy.

Had Life Changer been mentioned only in a one-time meeting, it would have had an impact, but the impact would have been temporary. The creation of the internal brand anchored the emotional impact of the need for safety into the company's DNA. M2Z and Life Changer became powerful internal brands. Every employee knew what they stood for:

- Taking ownership of their job

- Making value-based decisions

- Calling a critical and life-saving time-out

It is also important to note that WM senior management's willingness to step up, accept accountability, and commit to working toward a culture of zero safety failures speaks volumes about organizational courage. In our experience, there are too few companies willing to admit fault and openly resolve to do something about it. After Life Changer, few doubted WM's commitment to take the right action. There was enormous positive impact among all stake-holders, especially employees. When they saw the company walk the talk and live the values, it greatly accelerated the safety culture transformation as people inside personalized and started to defend the new culture. The impact quickly spread to others in the industry.

A vibrant culture empowers employees to use their judg-ment to arrive at the right result. This is rarely accomplished through policy manuals or handbooks. Instead, it is accom-plished through the "tribal" wisdom of the organization, where cultural behavior is transferred from one employee to the next through shared stories and behavior. Created with the input of every level of your company, your brand will become a visual affirmation of your values and how your employees must conduct themselves in your organization.

Once your internal brand is established, consider expanding the brand to safety-specific functions. The brand conveys how employees should approach a particular task or operation. Jetco uses this motto for their drivers: "Follow the car in front of you as if your loved ones were in it." Inviting them to imagine their family near them on the road is personal, not an extension of some rule or regulation.

Use your imagination and creativity, and the vision and talents of your team, to create any visual reminder related to safety. In your development of a culture of prevention, these tools can pay off for your company in ways that words alone never will. Here are a few examples:

INTERNAL SAFETY BRANDS

You are accountable for ensuring safe outcomes.

Proceed with a safety-sensitive assignment only after assessing all possible risks.

Safety and service excellence are not mutually exclusive. We must be safe and productive. It is not an "either/or" proposition.

Drive pride among our front line employees.

CHAPTER 22:

Let Your Front Lines Write the Handbook

Tell me, and I will forget. Show me, and I may remember.
Involve me, and I will understand.
—Chinese Proverb

As you set out to establish or revise your safety policies and procedures, consult your front lines. They know where the real safety risks lie and what to do about them. Give them an opportunity to share their experiences, observations, and what they think management and the entire team needs to do differently. Listen to their input and validate them for caring enough about safety to speak up.

Empower your staff to write company manuals. This idea is especially effective with creating or updating safety manuals. Your people often know best how to establish guidelines that will ensure safety for all fellow employees. Let them outline those guidelines so that they can take ownership of the process. In writing the details of safety operations, your people are extending critical information not only to their peers but to new employees down the road. That long-term impact will reinforce the importance of what they are doing.

When the Jetco front lines wrote their handbook, the team defined different topics and brought in different internal subject-matter experts. There was always a scribe in the room—an outstanding writer. Jetco's handbook now is simple; it's written in a one- or two-paragraph form, and it's full of pictures so the handbook is a visual. The beautiful aspect is that if somebody comes to Brian now and says,

"Why do we have this in our handbook?" he gets to say, "The ideas in this handbook aren't set in stone. What was a good idea two years ago may no longer be a good idea. Let's talk about what needs to be improved, and let's rewrite it." It's living and breathing. That's the essence of a good handbook—your team owns it and keeps it alive.

CHAPTER 23:

How to Kill Normalization of Deviance

In chapter 6, we addressed safety dysfunctions. One of the critical dysfunctions is normalization of deviance. As we stated, this is when people within an organization become accustomed to shortcuts and deviant behaviors in the conduct of their work. Over time, with no consequence for the deviations, the shortcuts become the norm. People involved inside the organization fail to recognize the danger of the new normal. How do we drive normalization of deviance out of our safety cultures?

Perhaps the most impactful training video that Brian has used for the Jetco team is entitled *Stopping Normalization of Deviance* by Astronaut Mike Mullane (mikemullane.com). This is a video that everyone in safety-sensitive businesses, from the front lines to the C-suite, must watch. Mullane advises companies to employ these tools to stop normalization of deviance in its tracks:

- **Do not allow shortcuts.** Budget and production pressures often force people to take a shortcut. Here's the problem: the shortcut will usually work. Because it worked, team members will be tempted to take the shortcut over and over again, and the shortcut becomes the norm. As a common example, an employee can get away with not wearing personal protective equipment, and nothing will generally happen—until that one tragic day.

- **Maintain best practices.** "How come we never have the time and money to do it right, but there is always time and money to do it over?" Leaders must rigidly maintain best practices in order to ensure that the organization executes properly the first time. Mullane points out that there are three steps to this process: building a plan, training, and execution. The first two steps are easy. We write our plans and teach in a controlled environment. There are few variables in the boardroom or class-room. The issue is in execution. In a healthy safety culture, there is recognition that normalization of deviance is prevented by how we execute on a daily basis. We have handbooks. We are trained. None of that matters if we do not maintain our best practices without compromise.

- **Allow time-outs for employees to adapt to their environment.** As stated above, our training occurs in a static environment. In the real world, circumstances change by the minute. Employees must understand that the situation determines the behavior. Here is an example we have all faced: The speed limit is sixty-five mph on a highway. If we drive into blinding rain or a snow storm, does that mean we maintain our speed of sixty-five mph? Of course not. Unforeseen and unpredictable events occur all of the time. This is why, in chapter 5, we strongly encourage employees to report near misses and call time-outs without fear of reper-cussion. Sometimes the environment changes so fast that the employee needs time to regroup or consult with management or a peer. If we do not institutionally encourage these time-outs, we are without doubt promoting the normalization of deviance, intentionally or not.

- **Keep an open mind.** When performing root cause investigations, as outlined in chapter 20, do not begin with the end in mind. Oftentimes, we perform a root cause investigation with a preconceived notion as to the cause. Such a preconception may cause us to look in all of the wrong places. It may be that the root cause is staring at us from the mirror. While that can be uncomfortable, we are going after the truth, wherever it may lead us.

- **Include time for reflection.** In meetings, review what is working (best practices) and what is not working (worst practices). Look for signs of drift. Never allow employees to have an attitude of "We've always done it this way." In chapter 22, we advised you to let your employees write the handbook. This is so they have ownership of the best practices. Recognize, however, that the best ideas can become outdated. Employees are less likely to follow a practice that no longer makes sense. If they are allowed to ignore one practice, then you have established a slippery slope. It is a far better idea to periodically review best practices and push the reset button. Decide what practices are still working and what practices are in need of revision. If a best practice is in place (outdated or not), it must be followed. Then, over time, the outdated practices must be edited or deleted to reflect the current reality.

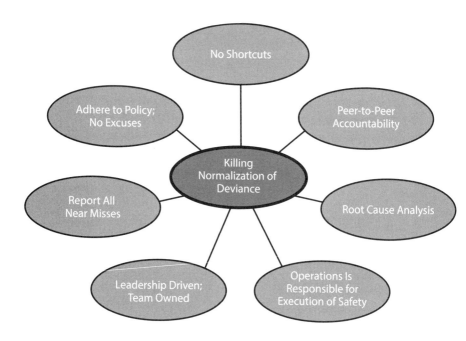

CHAPTER 24:
The Culture Contract:
A Simple Written Affirmation

As your company's culture, values, and code of conduct solidify, it is important to have written documentation. We are not talking about a heavy-duty handbook. Instead, we recommend a simple, one-page commitment. This is a "culture contract" between your employees and the company.

Take Jetco's "Driving to Perfection" commitment as an example:

DRIVING TO PERFECTION
MY COMMITMENT

Driving to Perfection embodies who we are as a company. D2P is a constant reminder of Jetco's core values and beliefs, and it guides our every action.

As a member of the Jetco team, I commit:

- To live and embrace our core values: Safety, Honesty, Integrity, Respect, Teamwork, Communication and Accountability. I will never compromise these values for any reason.

- To put safe operations above all else. "Zero" is the only acceptable result when measuring accidents and injuries. Through my actions, Jetco will achieve "Zero."

- To follow the car in front of me as if my family and loved ones are in it. I will always keep my distance and adjust my speed and space under the circumstances. I recognize that safety is my responsibility and a core value I will never compromise.

- To fully appreciate the risk of my job. I will plan and anticipate. I will always wear my PPE and be fully aware of my surroundings.

- To eliminate all distractions when driving or performing any other safety-sensitive function.

- To take my time and "do it right." I am empowered to call a time out for any safety concern, and I will support any person that stops work activities for any safety concerns.

- To report all near misses and accidents, no matter how minor. I recognize that every accident must be treated the same and that a minor accident only means I was lucky.

- To help myself and my team continuously improve through clear and consistent communication.

- To remember that safety stems from my behavior.

- To take care of myself and my equipment.

By signing this contract, I understand my role at Jetco. I accept my responsibility to create a safe environment for the entire Jetco team. With my commitment, we are Driving to Perfection!

_____   _____
Jetco Team Member   Manager

_____
Print Name

5521 Harvey Wilson Drive | Houston, Texas 77020 | 713.676.1111 | **jetcodelivery.com**

This written affirmation is essential because we are all human. We will have bad days when our behaviors deviate from company values. When coaching an employee who deviated from our core values, we encourage managers to pull the culture contract out of the file. When we meet with the wayward employee, we remind him or her of our values and of how we operate at our company. We also remind the employee that we all agreed on a code of conduct in writing. Normally, this reminder is all the employee needs, and it is much more effective than overused disciplinary tactics such as write-ups and suspensions.

As you can see from this example, the contract is focused on safety-sensitive functions. (After all, when driving eighty-thousand-pound loads around the city, safety is paramount.) Your company's cultural contract should capture the nonnegotiable values and behaviors required for an employee to thrive in your company. Anything more than one page will dilute your message and become over-kill.

Your culture contract is your written bond with your employees. It eliminates the chance for anyone (from the front line to the executive office) to use the excuse that he or she was not informed about those items that are most precious to your business.

CHAPTER 25:

Use Technology to Drive Safe Behavior

Jetco installed GPS in all our trucks in 2008. In 2015, the company installed cameras that look inside the cab and outside the window. GPS is a full onboard electronic recording system, which means the company has access to all kinds of critical data (e.g., speed, sudden braking and acceleration, and equipment utilization and production).

In both cases, two results happened: First, Jetco had a handful of employees who vehemently objected to the installation of this technology. A few resigned. Second, we had an undisputed cause and effect between the deployment of technology and accident reduction.

Think about this for a minute: If an employee objects to properly using technology, what are they afraid of? What are they doing with *your* equipment, *your* reputation, and *your* accident risk? If any employees vehemently object to the use of technology to monitor behavior, their actions (if not their words) prove a lack of accountability and should lead you to question whether those employees belong on your team.

With every technology-driven change, rumors and myths will erupt. This is perfectly normal. Anticipate the objections, and be ready with transparent answers. Bring in key employees from the front lines (i.e., your opinion leaders) to help vet and implement the technology. Be respectful of the process.

In the end, you cannot let the naysayers curtail your use of technology to monitor behavior. Let's also get rid of the myth that technology is too expensive. The opposite is true—it is too costly *not* to deploy safety technology.

However, it would be too simplistic to just ignore employee concerns, even though your decision for employee technology is not negotiable. It comes down to effective change management. Here are a few ideas to address the fears that often accompany change:

- **Offer empathy.** We anticipated and understood the possible concerns. Major change is frightening for many employees, so we acknowledged the legitimacy of the worry. Being empathetic is a way to let your team know you are not deaf to their concerns.

- **Over-communicate.** Jetco selected a handful of employees to be on our beta team—including some of the most vocal opponents to the change. We kept this axiom in mind: "Those who participate are likely to support. Those who are excluded are likely to oppose." Jetco built supporters by bringing them inside.

As the beta team became comfortable with the process change, they spread the word. They addressed our teams' fears in ways that had greater credibility than Brian could ever garner.

Technology is part of Jetco's DNA. It has been a success in every respect. Brian made a unilateral, nonnegotiable decision, and it turned out to be the right one. More importantly, he recognized that the battle would be won or lost in how we *implemented* the change—not in the change itself.

As a leader, you must stand up for what you believe is right. Some decisions will not be up for discussion. However, by being empathetic while carefully defining the implementation process around the change that you desire to create, you can convert opponents to allies. If your vision was correct, the team will come to support and respect it.

CHAPTER 26:

Shock and Awe

In our experience, accidents and injuries are not spread out evenly throughout the year. For some unexplained reason, they come in waves. If you have experienced a long period of relative safety and tranquility, the waves can overwhelm the leadership and front lines of the company. The first reaction may be, "It was minor. We were perfect for so long that we were due for some adversity." While not an acceptable reaction, it is an entirely human one. This reaction may carry over to the next few incidents as well, especially if they are minor. At some time, however, you need to realize that your organization is talking to you. Something is amiss.

When Brian was in the recycling business, his mentor, Harry Pelz, would walk through the production plant. He would immediately look at the corners of the plant. If the corners were clean and organized, that was a sign that the plant manager was running a good operation and watching the details. If the corners were messy and a catch-all for the plant's waste, he knew that there were deeper problems. That was his quick check, and it worked 100 percent of the time. Our quick check is safety results.

Safety outcomes are nothing more than the product of a well-run operation. If safety outcomes are poor, it is likely that there are deeper problems in the company.

So, when you hit a wave of safety problems, you have to dig deeper and review the broader operations. You are certain to find defects somewhere along the chain—leadership deficiencies, normalization of deviance, hiring

issues, orientation or training problems, or unclear understanding of company processes among employees. Even
if the wave of safety problems results in only minor injuries or costs, you still must dig deeper. Always remember
that severity is simply a function of whether or not you got
lucky.

In the face of a series of safety failures, you have to
shock the system. This means taking an unconventional
action, one that is not a part of your every-day (or every-
year) repertoire. The shock is a quick and aggressive hit that
cannot be mistaken for a part of your normal safety function. The team is seeing you sweat, and they are going to
sweat as hard, if not harder, than you. That's what world-
class organizations do, big or small. Jim tells a story of the
US Air Force taking aggressive action during his days as a
military pilot by standing down an entire fleet of airplanes
in response to a series of unfavorable safety incidents. Air
crews were required to participate in special safety inter-
ventions to get refocused before they were allowed to fly
again.

In a more current example, Jetco experienced a wave
of safety failures in a short period of time. They all seemed
unrelated—different incidents, different operating units,
different root causes. There wasn't time to connect the
dots. We needed to act fast. There would be time for reflection later.

To shock the system, we announced that we were shutting the company down—that if we could not execute safely
then we would not execute at all. All of a sudden, we had
everyone's attention. Shutting down? What about my job?
How can I fix that? In connection with the shutdown, here is
the memo we sent:

Team,

The rash of safety failures is out of control. Because of this, we are shutting down the company on Monday until you have participated in a required operational safety meeting. If we can't do our jobs safely, we won't do our jobs at all.

This means no driver will be dispatched and no one will be allowed in the office, shop, or warehouse to work until you attend a mandatory shut-down meeting.

We're going to discuss what is going on and how we're going to get this right. At the conclusion of the meeting, each of you will be asked to sign a commitment form, recommitting to safe behavior.

That form must be turned in to your manager before you will be allowed to return to work. Again, no one works until they attend this meeting.

In essence, the shutdown grabbed everyone's attention. The mere gesture of taking a time-out and shutting down operations to get the team realigned is a serious and bold statement that leaves no doubt that management is serious about safety as a core value. While we did not close the company (we are not foolish), we did in fact shut everyone out from their jobs until they attended a mandatory meeting. We limited the size of the meetings to ten people. There was no lecture. We posted the accident photos and let the team talk. We made them personally own the accidents. It is one thing to describe an accident and another to be confronted with photos and forced to react—to discuss what went wrong and to personally commit to change their behavior.

Here are the instructions Brian gave to his session leaders, which he called "The Sound of Silence":

Team,

When you execute the meetings on Monday, remember that silence creates discomfort. As the session leaders, you might be tempted to lecture or break the silence. Don't!

Start the meeting by showing the photos. Then go back to each photo (or incident), one by one. Ask the following of the attendees: What did you see? What would you have done? This dent on the car looks pretty minor, so why are we talking about it? The team should come to the conclusion that the dent could have been a fatality.

You see the point: Ask the questions. Let the team talk. Silence is your friend.

If no one talks, then just sit there. Let it be silent till someone does. Also, ensure that no one person is dominating. If you have ten people in the room, all ten must talk. Talking creates ownership. You must not solve the problems for the team. And, if the team does not figure out and own these issues, then that tells us that we have a lot more work to do—quickly. The less you say as session leaders, the more you will learn.

In March 2016, the Washington, DC, metro rail shut down completely for a full day for emergency safety inspections. Even though he knew that the shutdown would anger and inconvenience many commuters, Metro General Manager Paul Wiedefeld put safety above all else. Shutting down an entire metro system in one of the country's largest markets in the name of safety is a tremendous example of "shock and awe." At the same time, Wiedefeld established himself as a courageous leader, one who clearly put the safety value above any other operational priorities. In an article entitled "After shutdown, Metro riders ask what's next," *The Washington Post*'s Robert Thomson wrote: "Wiedefeld's response to the cable problem may have signaled something bigger about his approach to the job. The extraordinary shutdown showed that he's willing to do things differently. That could include a rethinking of the entire rebuilding strategy that Metro has employed for the past five years."

There will come times in every company's life cycle where "shock and awe" is needed. Think now about your "shock and awe" plan. When that time comes, you won't have the luxury of time to plan. You will have to move immediately into execution mode so that the company can return to safety excellence.

CHAPTER 27:

Life-Critical Rules:
No Excuses and No Explanations

If we visited your company and asked any employee, "What are your life-critical rules?" how would they answer? Do you have published life-critical rules? In the simplest terms, a life-critical rule is one that, if violated, could kill or seriously injure the employee or any third person. These are the rules that if violated will lead to immediate termination or, at the very least, suspension without pay. Immediate termination is what should normally result. What should you define as your life-critical rules? It all depends on the greatest risks in your business. Life-critical rule candidates might include equipment lock out or tag out, following too closely in a vehicle, failure to use seat belts and back up alarms on a forklift . . . and the list goes on.

You likely know your own life-critical rules, and your insurance carriers can help. However, resist the urge to dictate these rules; the real knowledge comes from your team. Consider explaining the importance of life-critical rules to your team. Then, let the team identify what they believe to be the most critical ones. Tally the votes, and we can assure you that your team will have identified all or almost all of your life-critical rules. Once the rules are identified, they can be communicated in a number of different ways—wallet cards, posters, and training sessions, to name a few. The team's ownership of the rules should be strong; after all, they identified and developed them. As an example, when the Jetco team recently engaged in this exercise, they determine the following most common ideas:

failure to use seat belts, school zone violations, failure to perform pre-trip and post-trip inspections, illegal cell phone use while driving, and speed or space management (i.e., improper following distance).

Once the rules are published and everyone understands them, you must revise your policies to indicate that these violations will have their own set of consequences apart from your normal processes. Now for the really hard part: What if an employee violates the life-critical rule? Are you prepared to act? What if the employee is tenured or otherwise has a good safety record? If employees see selective enforcement of these rules, the rules *and you* will lose credibility. There must be a level playing field and equal enforcement. We understand how difficult this can be. If it is any comfort, remind yourself that most life-critical violations are made at the choice of the employee. These rules are not ones that can be ignored by error or omission. They involve a deliberate decision to act recklessly. So, if that is how the employee feels about his or her safety and that of those around them, what do you really owe this employee? You are doing your organization and the employee a favor by acting aggressively. And as for the employee's past safety record, were they good, or were they lucky?

Here are Jetco's life-critical rules. What would your life-critical rules look like?

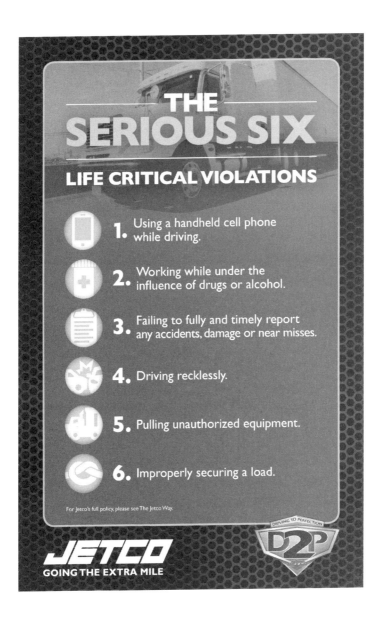

CONCLUSION:

Who Packs Your Parachute?

Jim tells this powerful story in his keynote presentations based on a pivotal personal experience early in his professional life. This story underscores the importance of recognizing the significance of our team members and of not believing that our titles make us better than our front lines.

The son of parents from a small Ohio town, both from long-established working-class families, I was blessed to be raised in a home with a strong blue-collar ethic. My grandfathers and uncles were all frontline railroad employees—conductors, engineers, and mechanical car men. My great-grandfather died on the job when a railroad boxcar fell from its jacks and crushed him underneath while he was working as a mechanical repair laborer. My father provided for us as a house painter in the Arizona desert around Phoenix.

I grew up with an appreciation for the value of the blue-collar work ethic. I developed a special understanding of those who toil without complaint in the shadows, with little glory or recognition.

As it was, I was the first on either side of the family to graduate from a university. During my time at school, I developed an interest in flying fast airplanes. After four years of basic military leadership training, academic testing, and thorough physical exams, I was selected upon college graduation to attend US Air Force jet pilot flight training.

This was pretty heady for a kid from the working class—selection for Air Force jet pilot school. It was a rigid and extensive selection process with only a handful selected out of every hundred applicants in those days. Once commissioned on active duty and processed, it was on to a base in Texas for flight school. The competition was stiff. Everyone there had gone through similar screening just to get an appointment.

The curriculum was pressure packed and aggressive. Sweat is a great solvent, and program washout rates were high as the training deepened. In my class, we started training with fifty-seven officers, but by the end of the fifty-three-week crucible, only twenty of the original cadre remained standing to be awarded the silver wings of an Air Force pilot.

I was on a mission. I applied myself, did well in all phases, and graduated in the top 10 percent of the class. Based on academics, flying scores, and physical fitness, I secured a much-coveted slot flying the highly sophisticated top-of-the-line jet fighter of the era—the supersonic Mach 2+ F-4 Phantom II—so it was off to Phantom school. There the competition was manifold. Everyone there was at the top of the pyramid, which made for extraordinary comradeship and a good deal of professional aloofness.

Somewhere in the journey from leaving home to that assignment flying an F-4, I lost my way. I was set up for a humbling lesson. One day early in my service tenure, walking down the street on base I saw an enlisted man in his utility uniform on the other side of the street walking toward me. He was about my age. I didn't acknowledge him . . . I was a fighter pilot. I flew the Phantom. He was an enlisted man. I didn't think I had anything to say to him. After all, I was at the top of the food chain . . . or so I thought.

He crossed the street, walked right up to me, gave me a salute, and said, "Sir, you are Lt. Schultz."

"Yes, who are you?" I replied.

"Sir, I am Sergeant Winslow. I am part of the 426th with you," he said.

"Sgt. Winslow, I don't recognize you. What do you do in the 426th?" I asked.

He replied, "Sir, I am in life support. I am responsible for packing your parachute."

He packed my parachute! If something went wrong while I was in the jet and needed to jettison my airplane, my life depended upon him doing his job well. And I had never given him the time of day? How Sgt. Winslow did his job may well have determined whether or not I made it home that day, whether I was able to raise my children, whether I was able to walk on solid ground again. Yet, in my own self-absorbed way, I let ego overcome my blue-collar sensibilities. Somehow I thought anyone not flying a fighter jet was unworthy of my time. Never had I taken the time to notice or appreciate those, such as Sgt. Winslow, who were critical to my life. How could I forget that I was a member of a team and that I was standing on the shoulders of people who labored every day in the trenches just so I could succeed?

It was a momentous, life-changing lesson for me. It made me realize that people pack my parachute every day in so many ways. We can never forget the power of the people around us. Leading people is a higher calling. So the question is, "Who packs your parachute every day?"

REFERENCES

1. James O'Toole and Warren Bennis, "A Culture of Candor," *Harvard Business Review*, June 2009.

2. Edelman, "Activating Communications Marketing -- Promoting, Protecting & Evolving Reputation," Corporate Reputation Presentation, 2015.

3. Stephen M. R. Covey, "How the Best Leaders Build Trust," *LeadershipNow/M2 Communications*, 2009, http://www.leadershipnow.com/CoveyOnTrust. html.

4. Deborah Schroeder-Saulnier, "Employee Engagement: Leading the Way to an Engagement Culture," Right Management/Linkage, 2008.

5. Cody Likavec and Laura Troyani, "The TINYpulse 2015 Employee Engagement & Organizational Culture Report," TINYpulse, 2015.

6. National Transportation Safety Board Aircraft Accident Report (AAR-14/01), "Descent Below Visual Glidepath and Impact With Seawall; Asiana Airlines Flight 214; Boeing 777-200ER, HL7742; San Francisco, California; July 6, 2013," June 24, 2014.

7. Diane Vaughan, *The* Challenger *Launch Decision: Risky Technology, Culture, and Deviance at NASA* (Chicago: University of Chicago Press, 1996).

8. William Bruce Cameron, *Informal Sociology: A Casual Introduction to Sociological Thinking* (New York: Random House, 1963).

9. John P. Kotter, *Leading Change* (Boston: Harvard Business School Press, 1996).

10. PEP is a trademark of Master Connection Associates G-Force (courtesy of Mike "Pags" Pagano).

11. Category definition content courtesy of K. Scott Griffith, SG Collaborative Solutions.

ADDITIONAL REFERENCES

We are often asked about our favorite business books. These are a few on our short list that we like and recommend:

Bethune, Gordon and Scott Huler. *From Worst to First*. New York: John Wiley & Sons Inc., 1998.

Bossidy, Larry and Ram Charan. *Execution: The Discipline of Getting Things Done*. New York: Crown Business, 2002.

Ellis, Lee. *Leading with Honor: Leadership Lessons from the Hanoi Hilton*. Cumming: FreedomStar Media, 2012.

Fielkow, Brian L. *Driving to Perfection: Achieving Business Excellence by Creating a Vibrant Culture.* Minneapolis: Two Harbors Press, 2013.

Kotter, John P. *Leading Change*. Boston: Harvard Business School Press, 1996.

Lencioni, Patrick. *The Advantage: Why Organizational Health Trumps Everything Else in Business*. San Francisco: Jossey-Bass, 2012.

Novak, David. *Taking People with You: The Only Way to Make Big Things Happen*. New York: Portfolio, 2013.

Whitehurst, Jim. *The Open Organization: Igniting Passion and Performance*. Boston: Harvard Business Review Press, 2015.

ABOUT THE AUTHORS

Brian and Jim have been close colleagues and friends for over a decade. They worked side-by-side as senior executives for trucking giant Waste Management Inc. (WM), the largest environmental/solid waste company in North America. Since then, they have worked together on a number of projects bringing transformational change to underperforming organizations and helping healthy organizations reach new heights.

Jim and Brian both deliver keynote addresses and workshops around the topics of building healthy organizational culture and safety excellence. They may be contacted as provided below.

Raised in Arizona, Jim's professional life resulted in many relocations around the US and overseas. He has been married for forty-five years to Constance, and they have three adult children and six grandchildren. They currently reside in the central Texas Hill Country.

Raised in Wisconsin, Brian holds a B.A. from the University of Wisconsin–Madison and a J.D. from Northwestern University Law School. He has spent his professional career in Milwaukee and Houston. Brian has been married for twenty-six years to Cheryl, and they have three children. They currently reside in Bellaire, Texas.

ABOUT JAMES T. SCHULTZ

Jim is a well-established senior executive with over forty years successful hands-on experience leading transformational change in complex organizations. Early in his life he developed a passion for excellence while serving as a supersonic F-4 Phantom II jet fighter pilot in the US Air Force, where he acquired his "don't forget who packs your parachute" approach to leadership. Today, Jim leads his own consulting and coaching practice with clients in high-consequence operations.

Previously, Jim held various senior-level posts in both the private and public sectors, including executive vice president and chief administrative officer at Patriot Rail Company; senior vice president employee and customer engagement and vice president health and safety at trucking giant Waste Management Inc. (WM); and vice president and chief safety officer at the railroad CSX, where he was termed "culture change guru" by *Progressive Railroading Magazine* for leading a cultural reinvention after decades of adversarial labor union–company management interactions. Jim also offers a distinctly unique leadership perspective, having been appointed as the top career safety official for the Federal Railroad Administration (FRA), where he managed the nation's federal rail safety oversight and enforcement activities through a cadre of five-hundred-plus federal rail safety inspectors.

During his tenure at WM, Jim's "Mission to Zero" (M2Z) and "Life Changer" programs produced in five years a marked improvement in foundational safety culture in this international fifty-thousand-employee company, resulting in a dramatic 75 percent reduction in worker injuries and a 50-plus percent reduction in the corporation's annual workers' compensation costs.

Jim and his programs have been featured in print media, including *The Wall Street Journal*, *The Washington Post*, *Traffic World*, *The Journal of Commerce*, and other public and industry publications. He is highlighted in the leadership book *Red Zone Management* (Holland, 2001). He served as a rail safety spokesman on screen for TV news media outlets and as an expert consultant for ABC's *20/20*. He is the author of papers on rail safety, leadership, and culture, including several Reports to Congress.

Jim was a faculty lecturer in the European divisions of the University of Maryland and Central Texas College while stationed overseas in the Air Force. He was recognized with the civilian Silver Star for Bravery Award from the American Federation of Police for action while in the Air Force. Active in his community, Jim was formerly a member of the executive committee, chairman of the personnel committee, and a member of the board of directors for the Jacksonville Urban League.

Jim holds an FAA commercial pilot license certification with multi-engine jet and instrument ratings. He earned, in residence, a master's degree from Webster University, a bachelor's degree from Arizona State University, and completed post-graduate and executive leadership programs in residence at Harvard Business School, the University of Southern California, and Northwestern University.

Contact Jim:
jim@jimschultzgroup.com
LinkedIn: linkedin.com/in/jimschultzgroup

ABOUT BRIAN L. FIELKOW

Brian Fielkow is a seasoned executive with more than thirty years of experience in entrepreneurial leadership. He brings a wealth of expertise with particular strengths in workplace safety, creating sustained growth, a healthy company culture, decommoditizing products and services, employee engagement, strategic planning, and business development. Brian's background includes corporate law and extensive operations experience.

Currently, Brian is owner and CEO of Jetco Delivery, a $34 million-plus freight and logistics company based in Houston, Texas, which he purchased in 2006. Brian's business experience is entirely in safety-sensitive industries, and he is an expert in building behavior-based safety cultures. He believes that safety excellence results from employee engagement, behavior, philosophy, and attitude—much more than from rules and regulations.

Brian is the author of *Driving to Perfection: Achieving Business Excellence by Creating a Vibrant Culture* (Two Harbors Press, 2014), which is a how-to guide to growing a healthy company culture. Rather than focusing on theory, Brian provides hands-on tools for business leaders of any size organization to take their company to the next level and grow their bottom line through their company's culture. As an expert on corporate culture, Brian travels internationally helping business leaders develop their own tools for creating and anchoring their own company's culture. Brian has appeared on CBS, NBC, FOX, NPR, and VOA. His articles have been published by *Fast Company* and *TheStreet*, among others, and he is a regular contributor to Entrepreneur.com. He and his companies have been the recipients of numerous industry and business awards, including the Vistage Member Leadership Award, the Texas Trucking Association Grand Champion Award, inclusion in Inc. 5000's ranking of fastest growing companies, and designation as a top workplace by the *Houston Chronicle*.

From 1989 to 1996, Brian practiced corporate law with Godfrey & Kahn in Milwaukee, where he represented privately held companies in a variety of transactions, including joint ventures, acquisitions and divestitures, succession planning, corporate governance and buy-sell agreements, general contracts, venture capital, and financing transactions. In 1996, Brian joined one of his clients, the Peltz Group, as COO. Peltz was a major regional recycling company. When Waste Management purchased the company, Brian became executive vice president of Recycle America Alliance, a position that he held shortly before his purchase of Jetco Delivery.

Brian holds a BA from the University of Wisconsin–Madison and a JD from the Northwestern Pritzker School of Law.

Contact Brian:
brian@brianfielkow.com
brianfielkow.com
LinkedIn: linkedin.com/in/brianfielkow
Facebook: facebook.com/brianfielkow
Twitter: @Brian_Fielkow

ADDITIONAL PUBLICATIONS BY JAMES T. SCHULTZ

Jim Schultz is coauthoring *Healing The Dysfunctional Company: A Roadmap to Performance Excellence and Higher Profits* with longtime friend and former business colleague Charles E. "Chuck" Williams. This book, currently in pre-publication, addresses common organizational dysfunctions that creep into companies and rob efficiency, productivity, and ability to achieve maximum financial performance. *Healing The Dysfunctional Company* is due for release in 2017.

ADDITIONAL PUBLICATIONS BY BRIAN L. FIELKOW

Driving to Perfection: Achieving Business Excellence by Creating a Vibrant Culture

"Entrepreneur Fielkow urges fellow business leaders to harness the ultimate competitive weapon: company culture.

For Fielkow, building a company culture isn't a touchy-feely exercise but a 'hardcore business proposition.' A lawyer-turned–corporate executive, Fielkow bought the trucking firm Jetco Delivery in 2006 and set out to transform it into a world-class company. In his view, Jetco's competitive advantage isn't superior technology or having more trucks on the road. What sets Jetco apart is a culture based on well-defined values, employee empowerment and a commitment to excellence. 'An excellent culture occurs when people and process are in harmony with the company's vision and values,' he writes. Fielkow argues that too many leaders think culture is an undefinable entity or, worse, a waste of time. In fact, he says, culture is a 'strategic choice' that yields a measurable return on investment. To make his case, Fielkow shares his successes and failures in establishing Jetco's culture, cleverly summarized by the mantra 'Driving to Perfection.' Written in a succinct, amiable style, the book is a treasure trove of ideas on how to build a culture without spending a lot of money. Far from the superficial notions of culture often found in company brochures, Fielkow advances a sophisticated view of culture that permeates every aspect of business, from employee compensation to mergers and acquisitions. He spotlights a broad range of topics— leadership, communication, hiring, teamwork, accountability, etc.—and challenges many conventional business practices. For example, Jetco chooses to focus on its employees rather than blindly following a 'customer-first at any price' policy. Jetco's culture ensures workers are well-trained and empowered to take care of customers, which keeps them coming back with repeat business. Fielkow makes clear his distaste for lengthy employee handbooks, so he keeps his chapters brief and equipped with easy-to-skim lists. While culture-building may be inexpensive, Fielkow doesn't promise quick fixes. Developing a vibrant culture demands effort, and once achieved, it must be relentlessly guarded against complacency.

A smart, comprehensive guidebook steeped in the rough-and-tumble realities of business."

—*Kirkus Reviews*

Brian's published articles may be obtained at brianfielkow.com/press.

Brian offers training videos for purchase. These videos are accompanied by workshop modules so that purchasers can customize and apply the ideas in this book to their companies. To purchase a video, please visit: brianfielkow.com.

BULK PURCHASES OF *LEADING PEOPLE SAFELY*

For purchases of ten or more copies of *Leading People Safely*, please visit our website provided below and use the code LPSBulk at checkout. The discount will automatically be applied to single-transaction purchases of ten books or more. For purchases of one hundred books or more, please contact Jim and Brian for customized pricing. They may be reached via the means provided in the About the Authors section of this book.

http://brianfielkow.com/

PRAISE FOR JAMES T. SCHULTZ

"Because of the relationship he had developed with people in the rail industry, especially in labor . . . he proved to be a valuable asset . . . [he] led a change in corporate culture at CSX."

—Kathy Burns
***Florida Times-Union*, November 2000**

"He (Mr. Schultz) can help us create a company with a much higher degree of communication and openness that will become a model for the rail industry."

—A. R. "Pete" Carpenter
President and CEO, CSX Transportation
***The Journal of Commerce*, October 1997**

"Schultz's track record as a safety inspector was key . . . he impressed our management and impressed our president . . . we want to create change and Jim is an agent of change."

—Marty Fiorentino
***Tribune Washington Bureau*, 2000**

"Organizational reinvention has been a CSX priority since Jim Schultz joined the railroad as vice president, chief safety officer, and culture change guru."

—Pat Foran
***Progressive Railroading Magazine*, July 1999**

"Motivational speakers . . . such as James T. Schultz, a retired fighter pilot who's now the top gun for safety at CSX. He's a former top official at the Federal Railroad Administration which supervises rail safety . . . [said] that the new [just culture] approach holds the promise of improving safety . . . but also helps avoid labor strife—a big plus for keeping shippers happy."

—Chip Jones
***Richmond Times-Dispatch*, May 1999**

"[Chairman John] Snow hired FRA's safety chief, Jim Schultz, as CSX vice president for safety. Schultz, a serious-minded regulator who'd long been troubled by railroad labor relations, saw the real safety problem was CSX's labor–management culture. He set out with zeal to change it, and seemingly overnight CSX was transformed from a labor enemy to a labor darling."

—Don Phillips
***Trains Magazine*, March 2003**

"Within hours of the Cajon wreck, regional [Federal Railroad Administration] official Jim Schultz ordered dozens of investigators into the California desert for a safety blitz . . . Schultz's performance attracted notice at headquarters. He was soon promoted to the FRA's chief safety position in Washington."

—Don Phillips
***The Washington Post*, October 1996**

"Jim is an expert at culture change . . . he proved this first at CSX Corporation where he was integral in changing the way employees and management worked together that contributed to the company's success and improved job satisfaction for employees. During the past five years at our company . . . Jim has done more than improve our safety operation. With great effectiveness and enthusiasm, he has solidified a culture of safety leadership across the company. And he's accomplished that by engaging the entire workforce. He has become recognized by corporate America as a leader in safety and as a leader of men and women."

—David P. Steiner
President and CEO, Waste Management Inc.
Press release: Waste Management Inc., November 2005

"The course that Jim Schultz has set for us over the last three years to change the culture of our company has had a profound effect on our labor management relationships and has become a model for other companies to follow."

—Michael Ward
Chairman and CEO, CSX Corporation
***Florida Times Union*, November 2000**

"CSX Transportation recruited Jim Schultz, the fighter-pilot-cum-operating-officer who reasoned that if you sincerely treat employees as human assets—not intimidate them to conform—valuable creativity and loyalty will be unleashed."

—Frank Wilner
***Railway Age Magazine*, June 1999**

"A former Federal Railroad Administration chief safety officer, Jim Schultz, who later became a highly respected safety officer at CSX, is advising Los Angeles Metrolink as it moves to lead the rail industry in installing and implementing a positive train control system. Schultz won substantial praise at CSX during the late 1990s for his efforts to end the industry's 19th-century military legacy of top-down management engaging in employee harassment and intimidation to enforce safety rules and regulations. In its place, Schultz, a former Air Force fighter pilot and Chicago & North Western operating officer, advocated peer intervention and coaching within a progressive corporate culture that recognizes employees do not intentionally violate safety rules and regulations."

—Press Release: United Transportation Union, October 2010

"CSX's [CEO] Carpenter yesterday said that Mr. Schultz 'has built a well-deserved reputation as a zealous guardian of employee safety' and will make 'our safety team the best in the industry.'"

—*The Wall Street Journal*, October 1997

PRAISE FOR BRIAN L. FIELKOW

"Brian made a presentation and facilitated a workshop at our annual Safety Summit for about four hundred leaders in our company. Our company has had a Journey to Zero program for a couple of years now. We decided it was time to have someone from outside the company refresh the message. Brian took the time to learn about our business, challenges, and areas of outstanding performance. Throughout his presentation, he used real-world examples from his industry, as well as relating our company experiences to his message. He truly provided an energized significance to the Journey to Zero message, while providing some additional concrete concepts for improving employee safety programs.

"One of the measures of a great training is how people are applying the message when they get back to their everyday operations. It has been great to hear our managers and supervisors quoting from Brian's presentation and developing methods for implementing the ideas. His passion for safety performance was loud and clear throughout his presentation. It will be exciting to see our company put his ideas to work to continue with the Journey to Zero program."

—Tracy Bartels
Health and Safety Manager, Vail Resorts Inc.

"Brian spoke at the annual Southwest Movers Association conference. I particularly appreciated him sharing the ramifications of culture in the workplace, and I enjoyed sitting in on his session and taking note of the interest and active participation by the members. The members gave a major thumbs-up on his presentation and appreciated the opportunity to glean a great deal of helpful information from his presentation."

—John D. Esparza
President and CEO, Texas Motor Transportation
Association

"Brian's presentation to our management staff was a big hit! His approach to leadership and safety closely mirrors ours, and he is able to communicate it in a way that really hits home. He kept everyone's attention throughout and ended with a lively group discussion. His book is a great resource when implementing his ideas."

—Jeff Hakala
Vice President, Texas Ports, Ceres Gulf Inc.

"Brian was our speaker of choice this past year at our annual conference where he gave a presentation and hosted an interactive workshop for an audience of seventy-five people. Prior to his presentation, Brian took time to get to know our business, challenge areas, and areas of outstanding performance. This allowed him to tailor an impactful presentation and workshop to our audience's specific needs. Brian's message that safety and operations can work together to improve the overall company culture, all while continuing to grow the business, is exactly what we strive for. The feedback we received confirmed that his presentation was both relevant and engaging, and we continue to reiterate the messages that Brian taught us."

—Kathryn Mujezinovic
Vice President of Business Development, Link Staffing
Services

"Brian delivered his 'Driving to Perfection' keynote to the Houston Texans' business leadership team. At the Houston Texans, we realize that our culture is one of our keys to victory, but building a healthy culture is a journey without a finish line. Brian's presentation was engaging and relatable, and our team left with ideas that we will immediately implement to take our winning culture to an even higher level. Rather than offer platitudes that sound great but lack a "how to" component, Brian offered our team value-added tools that we will now adapt and implement as we enhance our internal culture. Whether you're running an NFL franchise, a Main Street business, or non-profit—and regardless of the size of your organization—Brian's keynote will help you create a championship culture for long term success."

—Jamey Rootes, President Houston Texans

"As a NASA employee, I was required to participate in many training sessions regarding leadership, project management, and safety. Brian's event beats them all. I know I will benefit greatly from the experience."

—Nicole Stott
Astronaut, retired, NASA

"What an experience! Brian Fielkow was the December luncheon speaker at our executive group. Brian is interesting, informative, inspirational, and impressive. He lives, breathes, and teaches culture, and not a single person left the room without having new ideas and action items to improve their organizations. It was a stellar way to close the year."

—Walter Ulrich
President and CEO, Houston Technology Center

"Brian delivered his Driving to Perfection (D2P) presentation and workshop at our TransLand executive planning session. We've been on a transformative journey for about two years, so his presentation was timely and helped our leaders connect the dots between their ideas for building a strong culture and Brian's proven techniques. We were impressed that with a brief amount of data, Brian could identify our culture killers and provide firm counsel on how to proceed. TransLand will most assuredly be implementing our personal brand of D2P thanks to outstanding guidance. Going into this session, I was concerned several members of my team would dismiss Brian's message. I'm pleased to report that not only did everyone receive the message well, they are excited to get it implemented at TransLand. I'm confident this is the recipe for us to break through to new levels of performance."

—Mark Walker
Chairman and CEO, TransLand